NINJA FOODI
SMART-LID
COOKBOOK

A Visual Guide to Air Frying, Pressure Cooking, Slow Cooking, and More for All Users

TESS M. STONE

TABLE OF CONTENTS

INTRODUCTION

The Ninja Foodi Smart Lid is a revolutionary new appliance that combines the functionality of a pressure cooker, air fryer, steamer, and more into one powerful machine. At its core is Ninja's innovative Smart Lid technology which allows you to unlock a wide array of cooking techniques with the simple turn of a valve.

So what exactly is the Smart Lid? It's an attachment lid that transforms your Ninja Foodi into a compact, all-in-one cooker. The Smart Lid features dual lids an air fry/stovetop lid and a removable pressure lid that locks into place. A smart valve in the center of the lid automatically adjusts and controls the pressure, temperature, and airflow within the pot based on the selected cooking function. This unique valve system is what allows the Smart Lid to switch effortlessly between pressure cooking, air frying, steaming, baking, searing, and more. For pressure cooking, the valve seals in heat and pressure for fast, flavorful meals. Flip it to the air fry position and it rapidly circulates hot air around your food for crispy, oven-fried textures without oil. The valve can also be opened to release pressure or to allow steam to escape for other cooking modes. The Smart Lid attaches securely to your Ninja Foodi inner pot, creating an airtight seal when pressure cooking. During air frying, the raised lid allows hot air to circulate while an ingenious drain in the lid catches excess fat and condensation. This dual lid system eliminates the need to change out lids or accessories you can pressure cook then air fry all in the same pot with no extra parts or pieces.

Using the Smart Lid is incredibly simple. Just install the appropriate lid, select your desired cooking function using the easy-to-read display panel, and the Smart Lid does the rest. It will automatically build the proper heat and pressure levels needed to achieve perfect results every time. The panel displays handy prompts to guide you through each step from preheating to releasing pressure. With the turn of the Smart Valve, you can cook everything from fall-off-the-bone ribs to crispy chicken wings to fluffy cakes and more. Pressure cooking tenderizes tough meats in a fraction of the time it takes an oven or stovetop. The air frying capabilities allow you to enjoy healthier fried foods without excess oil or mess. You can even use the Smart Lid to proof bread dough, steam vegetables, bake casseroles, dehydrate snacks, and make yogurt. The inner cooking pot is a heavy-duty, nonstick coated pot that is completely removable. This not only makes for easy cleanup, but you can sear, sauté, and brown ingredients right in the pot before switching to another cooking mode. The pot has an extra-large capacity to accommodate family-sized meals and is suitable for making everything from soups and stews to roasts and bakes.

When you're done cooking, the Smart Lid cleaning cycle gives you two options a quick clean for a light rinse or a deeper clean for tougher, baked-on messes. The inner pot, crisper basket, and other components are also dishwasher safe for ultimate convenience.

In essence, the Ninja Foodi Smart Lid takes all the functions of multiple kitchen appliances and combines them into one sleek, digital countertop device. Its innovative smart lid technology makes it incredibly easy to pressure cook, air fry, crisp, bake, steam, sear, and more with just the turn of a valve. No extra lids, pots, or accessories required! With the Smart Lid you can create an endless variety of fast, delicious meals with maximum versatility and minimum hassle.

BENEFITS OF SMART LID TECHNOLOGY

The Ninja Foodi Smart Lid offers an innovative multi-cooking solution that provides incredible versatility and convenience in the kitchen. Its smart lid technology brings a multitude of benefits that make cooking easier, healthier, and more efficient than ever before. One of the biggest advantages is the ability to use just one appliance for a wide variety of cooking techniques. With the simple turn of the Smart Valve, you can pressure cook, air fry, bake, sear, steam, dehydrate, and more. This eliminates the need for separate appliances cluttering your countertop and saves valuable kitchen space. Having all these functions in one place also makes meal preparation much more streamlined and efficient.

The Smart Lid technology also allows you to combine multiple cooking methods in ways that enhance flavor and texture. For example, you can pressure cook proteins to quickly tenderize them, then switch to air fry mode to crisp up the exterior to golden-brown perfection. Or bake a casserole, then broil the top to get a delicious flavor contrast. Combining functions like this was extremely difficult, if not impossible, with traditional kitchen appliances.

Another key benefit is the speed and efficiency of pressure cooking. Harnessing high-pressure steam allows you to cook foods up to 70% faster than traditional methods. Tough cuts of meat that would take hours in the oven are fall-off-the-bone tender in under an hour. You'll also save energy since pressure cooking requires less time and lower temperatures. This can substantially reduce your utility costs over time.

The Smart Lid's air frying capabilities offer a much healthier alternative to deep frying. Using rapid air circulation and precise temperature control, you can achieve delicious crispy textures with little to no oil required. This drastically reduces fat and calories compared to traditional fried foods while still providing that satisfying crunch. Air frying also eliminates messy oil splatters for much easier cleanup. The steam and bake functions provide versatile options for cooking vegetables, proteins, casseroles, breads, and more with moistness and flavor locked in. You can steam vegetables to tender perfection while preserving valuable nutrients. Or bake everything from meatloaves to cakes to artisan bread loaves using the precise temperature control.

For searing and browning, the Smart Lid's stove top mode allows you to quickly get a flavor-boosting sear on meats before slow cooking or braising. Or use it to caramelize onions and other aromatics to build layers of rich flavor. The sear function works in tandem with the other cooking modes for professional-level results.

The Smart Lid is incredibly user-friendly. The control panel walks you through each stage of cooking with clear prompts and messaging. This makes it easy for even novice cooks to master techniques like pressure cooking. The smart design also builds in handy safety features like automatic venting and overheat protection.

In addition to the basic functions, the Smart Lid offers specialty modes tailored for specific cooking tasks. These include DIY functions to proof bread dough, make yogurt, dehydrate snacks like beef jerky or dried fruit, and perform other specialty cooking jobs with ease. Cleaning and maintenance are simplified as well thanks to the Smart Lid. The self-cleaning cycle uses high heat and steam to dissolve and rinse away stubborn, baked on splatters and messes from the cooker's interior. The removable inner pot and other components are also dishwasher safe for ultimate convenience.

With the Ninja Foodi Smart Lid, you're getting an all-in-one cooking system that replaces multiple other appliances. This provides tremendous versatility to prepare a wide array of foods and dishes using a variety of techniques. The smart technology makes cooking easier and faster while unlocking new flavor possibilities. From crisping up foods with little oil to speeding up cook times, the Smart Lid has benefits that enhance both the process and the results of cooking delicious meals.

OVERVIEW OF COOKING FUNCTIONS

The Ninja Foodi Smart Lid is an incredibly versatile appliance that puts a multitude of cooking functions at your fingertips. With the simple turn of its smart valve, you can unlock different heat sources, airflow patterns, and pressure levels to execute a wide array of cooking techniques. Let's take a closer look at each of the core functions:

Pressure Cooking

This is perhaps the smartest and most powerful function of the Smart Lid. It allows you to harness high-pressure steam to cook foods up to 70% faster than traditional methods. The sealed pressure environment raises boiling point, allowing higher temperatures that break down tough fibers in proteins rapidly. This yields fall-off-the-bone tender results in a fraction of the time. Pressure cooking also locks in moisture, nutrients, and flavor that are often lost with other techniques. To pressure cook, you'll seal the Smart Lid and turn the valve to the "seal" position. The pot will build up the designated pressure level then start the programmed cook time. When done, you can rapidly release pressure or allow it to naturally release. The Smart Lid takes all the guesswork out of pressure cooking with presets for everything from ribs to risotto.

Air Frying

For crispy, crunchy textures without excessive oil, the air fry function can't be beat. It uses rapid air circulation and precise temperature control to achieve delicious fried texture and browning using little to no oil. The raised air fry lid allows air to rapidly circulate around your foods for even, allover crispness.   The key is the Smart Lid's air flow system and precision heating element which mimic the effects of deep frying using just hot air. Compared to deep frying, air frying drastically reduces fat and calories while still delivering that satisfying crunch. It's a healthier way to enjoy classic fried favorites like chicken, fries, and more.

Baking & Roasting

Bake everything from cakes and pies to roasted proteins with the Smart Lid's precise temperature control. For baked goods, the sealed baking environment ensures a moist, evenly-cooked interior with a perfect rise and texture. For roasting, the dry, steady heat yields juicy, flavorful meats and veggies in less time than an oven. The Smart Lid makes baking a breeze with preset functions for basic items like bread loaves or cakes, or you can customize settings to achieve the perfect "doneness" for specific recipes. You can even proof dough directly in the cooker before baking.

Broiling

This function uses intense, direct heat from the lid and pot to broil and char proteins or melt and crisp toppings. It mimics the intense radiant heat of your oven's broiler to quickly add a flavorful crust or sear in juices. The Smart Broil function is also perfect for recipes like au gratin dishes or baked dips where you want a beautifully browned, crispy top.

Steaming & Simmering

Using the cooker's steam function, you can gently steam vegetables, seafood, dumplings, eggs, and more to lock in moisture, color, and nutrients. The steam basket keeps foods suspended above the simmering liquid for delicate, even steaming. There are presets for tasks like making fluffy steamed eggs or dumplings. You can also simmer soups, sauces, and other recipes that require a gentle, low, steady temperature to develop flavor over time. The Smart Lid precisely controls and maintains the optimal simmer for perfect results.

Searing & Sautéing

The stove top function uses high heat from the inner pot surface to quickly sear proteins and sauté aromatics. This develops rich color, texture, and flavor before finishing with another cooking mode. The pot's nonstick coating is ideal for getting a flavorful sear on meats or caramelizing veggies and sauces. This preliminary searing step amp up the taste of braises, roasts, and other slow-cooked dishes.

Dehydrating

Using a precise combination of low heat and air flow, the dehydrate function allows you to make homemade snacks like beef jerky, dried fruit, veggie chips and more. It slowly removes moisture over several hours while maintaining an optimal dehydrating temperature. This function is also great for "recrisping" foods like fried items that have gone soggy.

These are just the core cooking capabilities the Smart Lid also offers specialized functions to make yogurt, proof bread dough, can foods, and much more. The possibilities are virtually endless with this one amazing appliance. With the Smart Lid you can truly master techniques and recipes that would normally require a full battery of kitchen equipment. Its smart technology makes all of these cooking functions as easy as the turn of a valve.

Overnight Oats with Fruit Compote

Prep: 10 mins | Cook: 0 mins | Serves: 2

Ingredients:

- US: 120g rolled oats, 240ml almond milk, 2 tablespoons maple syrup, 1 teaspoon vanilla extract, 100g mixed berries
- UK: 120g rolled oats, 240ml almond milk, 2 tablespoons maple syrup, 1 teaspoon vanilla extract, 100g mixed berries

Instructions:

1. In a bowl, combine rolled oats, almond milk, maple syrup, and vanilla extract.
2. Divide the mixture into two jars and refrigerate overnight.
3. In the morning, top with mixed berries fruit compote.

Nutritional Info: Calories: 250 | Fat: 4g | Carbs: 49g | Protein: 6g

Fluffy Frittata Cups

Prep: 15 mins | Cook: 20 mins | Serves: 6

Ingredients:

- US: 6 eggs, 60ml milk, 50g grated cheddar cheese, 50g diced bell peppers, 50g diced mushrooms, salt, pepper
- UK: 6 eggs, 60ml milk, 50g grated cheddar cheese, 50g diced bell peppers, 50g diced mushrooms, salt, pepper

Instructions:

1. Preheat the Ninja Foodi to 180°C.
2. In a bowl, whisk together eggs, milk, salt, and pepper.
3. Grease muffin tin cups and divide the egg mixture evenly.
4. Add diced bell peppers, mushrooms, and grated cheese to each cup.
5. Bake for 20 minutes or until set.

Nutritional Info: Calories: 120 | Fat: 8g | Carbs: 3g | Protein: 10g

Lemon Ricotta Pancakes

Prep: 15 mins | Cook: 10 mins | Serves: 4

Ingredients:

- US: 150g all-purpose flour, 1 tablespoon sugar, 1 teaspoon baking powder, 1/2 teaspoon baking soda, 240ml buttermilk, 1 egg, 100g ricotta cheese, zest of 1 lemon, butter (for cooking)
- UK: 150g all-purpose flour, 1 tablespoon sugar, 1 teaspoon baking powder, 1/2 teaspoon baking soda, 240ml buttermilk, 1 egg, 100g ricotta cheese, zest of 1 lemon, butter (for cooking)

Instructions:

1. In a bowl, mix flour, sugar, baking powder, and baking soda.
2. In another bowl, whisk buttermilk, egg, ricotta cheese, and lemon zest.
3. Combine wet and dry ingredients until just mixed.
4. Heat a nonstick pan over medium heat and add butter.
5. Pour 1/4 cup of batter per pancake onto the pan and cook until bubbles form, then flip and cook until golden.

Nutritional Info: Calories: 220 | Fat: 7g | Carbs: 30g | Protein: 9g

Sausage & Veggie Breakfast Casserole

Prep: 20 mins | Cook: 40 mins | Serves: 6

Ingredients:

- US: 6 sausages, 1 bell pepper (diced), 1 onion (diced), 6 eggs, 240ml milk, 100g shredded cheddar cheese, salt, pepper
- UK: 6 sausages, 1 bell pepper (diced), 1 onion (diced), 6 eggs, 240ml milk, 100g shredded cheddar cheese, salt, pepper

Instructions:

1. Preheat the Ninja Foodi to 180°C.
2. Cook sausages until browned, then slice them.
3. Sauté diced bell pepper and onion until soft.
4. In a bowl, whisk eggs, milk, salt, and pepper.
5. Layer sausages, veggies, and cheese in a baking dish, then pour egg mixture over.
6. Bake for 40 minutes or until set.

Nutritional Info: Calories: 290 | Fat: 18g | Carbs: 7g | Protein: 22g

Cinnamon Raisin Bread Pudding

Prep: 15 mins | Cook: 30 mins | Serves: 4

Ingredients:

- US: 4 slices of bread (cubed), 240ml milk, 2 eggs, 50g sugar, 1 teaspoon vanilla extract, 1/2 teaspoon ground cinnamon, 50g raisins
- UK: 4 slices of bread (cubed), 240ml milk, 2 eggs, 50g sugar, 1 teaspoon vanilla extract, 1/2 teaspoon ground cinnamon, 50g raisins

Instructions:

1. Preheat the Ninja Foodi to 160°C.
2. In a bowl, whisk together milk, eggs, sugar, vanilla extract, and cinnamon.
3. Add bread cubes and raisins, stirring until coated.
4. Pour mixture into a greased baking dish.
5. Bake for 30 minutes or until set and golden.

Nutritional Info: Calories: 220 | Fat: 5g | Carbs: 37g | Protein: 7g

Salmon & Cream Cheese Bagel Bombs

Prep: 15 mins | Cook: 20 mins | Serves: 4

Ingredients:

- US: 4 bagels, 200g smoked salmon, 100g cream cheese, 2 tablespoons chopped chives, salt, pepper
- UK: 4 bagels, 200g smoked salmon, 100g cream cheese, 2 tablespoons chopped chives, salt, pepper

Instructions:

1. Preheat the Ninja Foodi to 180°C.
2. Slice bagels in half and toast them.
3. Spread cream cheese on each half, then top with smoked salmon and chives.
4. Season with salt and pepper.
5. Bake for 10 minutes until warmed through.

Nutritional Info: Calories: 320 | Fat: 12g | Carbs: 38g | Protein: 18g

Maple Brown Sugar Oatmeal

Prep: 5 mins | Cook: 10 mins | Serves: 2

Ingredients:

- US: 100g rolled oats, 240ml water, 240ml milk, 2 tablespoons maple syrup, 2 tablespoons brown sugar, 1/2 teaspoon ground cinnamon
- UK: 100g rolled oats, 240ml water, 240ml milk, 2 tablespoons maple syrup, 2 tablespoons brown sugar, 1/2 teaspoon ground cinnamon

Instructions:

1. Combine oats, water, milk, maple syrup, brown sugar, and cinnamon in the inner pot.
2. Close the Ninja Foodi with the Smart-Lid and set to Pressure Cook on High for 5 minutes.
3. Once done, release pressure and stir well before serving.

Nutritional Info: Calories: 300 | Fat: 4g | Carbs: 56g | Protein: 9g

Mexican Chorizo & Egg Burritos

Prep: 10 mins | Cook: 15 mins | Serves: 4

Ingredients:

- US: 200g Mexican chorizo, 8 eggs (beaten), 4 large flour tortillas, 100g shredded cheese, salsa, avocado slices
- UK: 200g Mexican chorizo, 8 eggs (beaten), 4 large flour tortillas, 100g shredded cheese, salsa, avocado slices

Instructions:

1. Crumble chorizo into a skillet and cook until browned.
2. Add beaten eggs and scramble until cooked.
3. Divide the mixture onto warmed tortillas.

4. Top with shredded cheese, salsa, and avocado slices.
5. Roll into burritos and serve.

Nutritional Info: Calories: 420 | Fat: 26g | Carbs: 28g | Protein: 22g

Blueberry Streusel Muffins

Prep: 15 mins | Cook: 20 mins | Serves: 12

Ingredients:

- US: 250g all-purpose flour, 150g sugar, 2 teaspoons baking powder, 1/2 teaspoon salt, 120ml vegetable oil, 1 egg, 120ml milk, 200g blueberries
- UK: 250g all-purpose flour, 150g sugar, 2 teaspoons baking powder, 1/2 teaspoon salt, 120ml vegetable oil, 1 egg, 120ml milk, 200g blueberries

Instructions:

1. Preheat the Ninja Foodi to 180°C.
2. In a bowl, mix flour, sugar, baking powder, and salt.
3. In another bowl, whisk oil, egg, and milk.
4. Combine wet and dry ingredients, then fold in blueberries.
5. Spoon batter into muffin cups and sprinkle streusel on top.
6. Bake for 20 minutes or until golden.

Nutritional Info: Calories: 210 | Fat: 9g | Carbs: 30g | Protein: 3g

Breakfast Fried Rice

Prep: 15 mins | Cook: 10 mins | Serves: 4

Ingredients:

- US: 250g cooked rice, 4 slices bacon (chopped), 1 onion (chopped), 2 eggs (beaten), 100g frozen peas, 2 tablespoons soy sauce, 1 tablespoon sesame oil
- UK: 250g cooked rice, 4 slices bacon (chopped), 1 onion (chopped), 2 eggs (beaten), 100g frozen peas, 2 tablespoons soy sauce, 1 tablespoon sesame oil

Instructions:

1. In a skillet, cook chopped bacon until crispy, then remove and set aside.
2. Sauté chopped onion until translucent.
3. Push onions to the side and scramble beaten eggs.
4. Add cooked rice, frozen peas, cooked bacon, soy sauce, and sesame oil.
5. Stir-fry until heated through.
6. Serve hot.

Nutritional Info: Calories: 350 | Fat: 12g | Carbs: 45g | Protein: 14g

Buffalo Chicken Dip

Prep: 15 mins | Cook: 25 mins | Serves: 8

Ingredients:

- US: 2 cups cooked chicken (shredded), 1 cup cream cheese, 1 cup sour cream, 1 cup shredded cheddar cheese, 1/2 cup hot sauce, 1/4 cup ranch dressing, 1/4 cup chopped green onions, 1/4 teaspoon garlic powder, 1/4 teaspoon onion powder, salt, pepper, tortilla chips (for serving)
- UK: 450g cooked chicken (shredded), 225g cream cheese, 225g sour cream, 225g shredded cheddar cheese, 120ml hot sauce, 60ml ranch dressing, 4 green onions (chopped), 1/4 teaspoon garlic powder, 1/4 teaspoon onion powder, salt, pepper, tortilla chips (for serving)

Instructions:

1. Preheat your Ninja Foodi Smart-Lid to Air Crisp at 180°C (350°F).
2. In a mixing bowl, combine shredded chicken, cream cheese, sour cream, cheddar cheese, hot sauce, ranch dressing, green onions, garlic powder, onion powder, salt, and pepper.
3. Transfer the mixture to a baking dish suitable for the Ninja Foodi Smart-Lid.
4. Place the baking dish into the Ninja Foodi Smart-Lid and air crisp for 2025 minutes until bubbly and golden.
5. Serve hot with tortilla chips for dipping.

Nutritional Info: Calories: 280 | Fat: 22g | Carbs: 5g | Protein: 16g

Spinach Artichoke Dip

Prep: 10 mins | Cook: 20 mins | Serves: 6

Ingredients:

- US: 200g fresh spinach, 1 can (400g) artichoke hearts, 200g cream cheese, 1/2 cup sour cream, 1/2 cup mayonnaise, 1 cup shredded mozzarella cheese, 1/4 cup grated Parmesan cheese, 2 cloves garlic (minced), salt, pepper, tortilla chips or bread (for serving)
- UK: 200g fresh spinach, 1 can (400g) artichoke hearts, 200g cream cheese, 120ml sour cream, 120ml mayonnaise, 100g shredded mozzarella cheese, 25g grated Parmesan cheese, 2 cloves garlic (minced), salt, pepper, tortilla chips or bread (for serving)

Instructions:

1. Preheat your Ninja Foodi Smart-Lid to Bake at 180°C (350°F).
2. In a food processor, blend spinach and artichoke hearts until finely chopped.
3. In a mixing bowl, combine cream cheese, sour cream, mayonnaise, mozzarella cheese, Parmesan cheese, minced garlic, salt, and pepper.
4. Fold in the spinach and artichoke mixture until well combined.
5. Transfer the mixture to a baking dish suitable for the Ninja Foodi Smart-Lid.

6. Bake for 1520 minutes until bubbly and lightly browned on top.
7. Serve hot with tortilla chips or bread for dipping.

Nutritional Info: Calories: 220 | Fat: 18g | Carbs: 5g | Protein: 8g

Meatballs with Grape Jelly Sauce

Prep: 15 mins | Cook: 25 mins | Serves: 6

Ingredients:

- US: 500g ground beef, 1 egg, 1/4 cup breadcrumbs, 1/4 cup grated Parmesan cheese, 1/4 cup chopped parsley, 1 teaspoon garlic powder, 1 teaspoon onion powder, salt, pepper, 1 cup grape jelly, 1 cup BBQ sauce
- UK: 500g ground beef, 1 egg, 25g breadcrumbs, 25g grated Parmesan cheese, 15g chopped parsley, 1 teaspoon garlic powder, 1 teaspoon onion powder, salt, pepper, 240ml grape jelly, 240ml BBQ sauce

Instructions:

1. Preheat your Ninja Foodi Smart-Lid to Sauté at medium heat.
2. In a mixing bowl, combine ground beef, egg, breadcrumbs, Parmesan cheese, parsley, garlic powder, onion powder, salt, and pepper. Mix until well combined.
3. Shape the mixture into meatballs.
4. Sauté the meatballs in the Ninja Foodi Smart-Lid until browned on all sides, about 810 minutes.
5. In a separate bowl, mix grape jelly and BBQ sauce.
6. Pour the grape jelly sauce over the meatballs.
7. Close the Ninja Foodi Smart-Lid and cook on Pressure Cook mode for 10 minutes.
8. Once done, let the pressure release naturally for 5 minutes before quick releasing.
9. Serve the meatballs hot as a delicious appetizer.

Nutritional Info: Calories: 350 | Fat: 15g | Carbs: 40g | Protein: 20g

Chicken Wings (Buffalo, BBQ, etc)

Prep: 10 mins | Cook: 30 mins | Serves: 4

Ingredients:

- US: 1 kg chicken wings, 1/2 cup hot sauce (for Buffalo wings), 1/2 cup BBQ sauce (for BBQ wings), 1/4 cup melted butter, salt, pepper, ranch or blue cheese dressing (for dipping)
- UK: 1 kg chicken wings, 120ml hot sauce (for Buffalo wings), 120ml BBQ sauce (for BBQ wings), 60ml melted butter, salt, pepper, ranch or blue cheese dressing (for dipping)

Instructions:

1. Preheat your Ninja Foodi Smart-Lid to Air Crisp at 200°C (400°F).
2. Season the chicken wings with salt and pepper.
3. Place the chicken wings in the Ninja Foodi Smart-Lid basket in a single layer.
4. Air crisp for 2530 minutes until crispy and golden brown, flipping halfway through.

5. For Buffalo wings: In a bowl, mix hot sauce and melted butter. Toss the cooked wings in the sauce until well coated.
6. For BBQ wings: Toss the cooked wings in BBQ sauce until well coated.
7. Serve hot with ranch or blue cheese dressing for dipping.

Nutritional Info: Calories: 320 | Fat: 22g | Carbs: 6g | Protein: 25g

Deviled Eggs

Prep: 15 mins | Cook: 10 mins | Serves: 6

Ingredients:
- US: 6 eggs, 1/4 cup mayonnaise, 1 teaspoon Dijon mustard, 1/2 teaspoon white vinegar, salt, pepper, paprika, chopped chives (for garnish)
- UK: 6 eggs, 60ml mayonnaise, 5ml Dijon mustard, 2.5ml white vinegar, salt, pepper, paprika, chopped chives (for garnish)

Instructions:
1. Place eggs in the Ninja Foodi Smart-Lid basket.
2. Add water to the inner pot until the eggs are just covered.
3. Close the lid and set to Pressure Cook for 5 minutes.
4. Once done, quick release the pressure and transfer the eggs to a bowl of ice water to cool.
5. Peel the eggs and slice them in half lengthwise. Remove the yolks and place them in a mixing bowl.
6. Mash the yolks with mayonnaise, Dijon mustard, white vinegar, salt, and pepper until smooth.
7. Spoon or pipe the yolk mixture back into the egg whites.
8. Sprinkle with paprika and garnish with chopped chives.
9. Serve chilled as a classic appetizer.

Nutritional Info: Calories: 80 | Fat: 7g | Carbs: 1g | Protein: 4g

Chili Lime Popcorn

Prep: 5 mins | Cook: 5 mins | Serves: 4

Ingredients:
- US: 1/2 cup popcorn kernels, 2 tablespoons olive oil, 1 teaspoon chili powder, 1 teaspoon lime zest, salt
- UK: 120ml popcorn kernels, 30ml olive oil, 5ml chili powder, 5ml lime zest, salt

Instructions:
1. Preheat your Ninja Foodi Smart-Lid to Air Pop at 200°C (400°F).
2. Add popcorn kernels and olive oil to the Ninja Foodi Smart-Lid basket.
3. Close the lid and air pop until all kernels are popped, about 35 minutes.
4. In a small bowl, mix chili powder, lime zest, and salt.
5. Toss the popped popcorn with the chili lime seasoning until evenly coated.
6. Serve immediately as a flavorful snack.

Nutritional Info: Calories: 120 | Fat: 7g | Carbs: 14g | Protein: 2g

Pretzel Bites with Beer Cheese

Prep: 20 mins | Cook: 12 mins | Serves: 6

Ingredients:

- US: 1 pound pizza dough, 1/4 cup baking soda, 4 cups water, coarse salt, 1 cup beer, 2 cups shredded cheddar cheese, 1 cup shredded mozzarella cheese, 2 tablespoons cornstarch, 1 clove garlic (minced), 1/2 teaspoon mustard powder
- UK: 450g pizza dough, 60ml baking soda, 950ml water, coarse salt, 240ml beer, 200g shredded cheddar cheese, 100g shredded mozzarella cheese, 30g cornstarch, 1 clove garlic (minced), 2.5ml mustard powder

Instructions:

1. Preheat your Ninja Foodi Smart-Lid to Bake at 200°C (400°F).
2. Roll out the pizza dough into a rectangle and cut into small squares to make pretzel bites.
3. In a large pot, bring water and baking soda to a boil.
4. Boil the pretzel bites in batches for 30 seconds, then remove with a slotted spoon and place on a parchment-lined baking sheet.
5. Sprinkle with coarse salt and bake for 1012 minutes until golden brown.
6. In a saucepan, heat beer over medium heat.
7. In a bowl, toss shredded cheddar and mozzarella cheese with cornstarch until coated.
8. Gradually add cheese mixture to the beer, stirring until melted and smooth.
9. Stir in minced garlic and mustard powder.
10. Serve pretzel bites hot with beer cheese dip.

Nutritional Info: Calories: 350 | Fat: 15g | Carbs: 35g | Protein: 15g

Stuffed Mushroom Caps

Prep: 15 mins | Cook: 20 mins | Serves: 4

Ingredients:

- US: 12 large mushroom caps, 1/2 cup breadcrumbs, 1/4 cup grated Parmesan cheese, 2 cloves garlic (minced), 2 tablespoons chopped parsley, 2 tablespoons olive oil, salt, pepper
- UK: 12 large mushroom caps, 25g breadcrumbs, 25g grated Parmesan cheese, 2 cloves garlic (minced), 15g chopped parsley, 30ml olive oil, salt, pepper

Instructions:

1. Preheat your Ninja Foodi Smart-Lid to Bake at 180°C (350°F).
2. Remove stems from mushroom caps and place them on a baking sheet.
3. In a bowl, mix breadcrumbs, Parmesan cheese, minced garlic, chopped parsley, olive oil, salt, and pepper.
4. Stuff each mushroom cap with the breadcrumb mixture.
5. Bake for 1520 minutes until mushrooms are tender and filling is golden brown.
6. Serve hot as a tasty appetizer.

Nutritional Info: Calories: 120 | Fat: 7g | Carbs: 10g | Protein: 5g

Caprese Skewers

Prep: 10 mins | Cook: 0 mins | Serves: 4

Ingredients:

- US: 12 cherry tomatoes, 12 small mozzarella balls, 12 fresh basil leaves, balsamic glaze, salt, pepper
- UK: 12 cherry tomatoes, 12 small mozzarella balls, 12 fresh basil leaves, balsamic glaze, salt, pepper

Instructions:

1. Assemble skewers by threading cherry tomatoes, mozzarella balls, and basil leaves onto toothpicks or skewers.
2. Arrange the skewers on a serving platter.
3. Drizzle with balsamic glaze and sprinkle with salt and pepper.
4. Serve immediately as a light and refreshing appetizer.

Nutritional Info: Calories: 90 | Fat: 6g | Carbs: 3g | Protein: 5g

Seven Layer Taco Dip

Prep: 15 mins | Cook: 0 mins | Serves: 8

Ingredients:

- US: 1 can (400g) refried beans, 1 cup sour cream, 1 cup guacamole, 1 cup salsa, 1 cup shredded cheddar cheese, 1 cup shredded lettuce, 1/2 cup diced tomatoes, 1/4 cup sliced black olives, tortilla chips (for serving)
- UK: 1 can (400g) refried beans, 240ml sour cream, 240ml guacamole, 240ml salsa, 100g shredded cheddar cheese, 50g shredded lettuce, 60g diced tomatoes, 30g sliced black olives, tortilla chips (for serving)

Instructions:

1. Spread refried beans evenly in the bottom of a serving dish.
2. Layer sour cream, guacamole, salsa, shredded cheddar cheese, shredded lettuce, diced tomatoes, and sliced black olives on top of the beans.
3. Serve with tortilla chips for dipping.
4. Enjoy this crowd-pleasing dip at your next gathering!

Nutritional Info: Calories: 220 | Fat: 15g | Carbs: 10g | Protein: 8g

Creamy Tomato Basil Soup

Prep: 10 mins | Cook: 25 mins | Serves: 4

Ingredients:

- US: 2 tablespoons olive oil, 1 onion (chopped), 2 cloves garlic (minced), 2 cans (28 oz each) whole peeled tomatoes, 1 cup vegetable broth, 1/2 cup heavy cream, 1/4 cup fresh basil (chopped), salt, pepper, grated Parmesan cheese (for garnish)
- UK: 2 tablespoons olive oil, 1 onion (chopped), 2 cloves garlic (minced), 2 cans (800g each) whole peeled tomatoes, 240ml vegetable broth, 120ml heavy cream, 1/4 cup fresh basil (chopped), salt, pepper, grated Parmesan cheese (for garnish)

Instructions:

1. Set the Ninja Foodi to 'Sear/Sauté' on medium heat. Add the olive oil and sauté the chopped onion until soft and translucent, about 5 minutes.
2. Add the minced garlic and cook for another minute.
3. Add the whole peeled tomatoes (with juice) and vegetable broth. Stir to combine.
4. Secure the pressure lid, set the vent to 'Seal,' and select 'Pressure Cook' on high for 10 minutes.
5. Quick release the pressure and remove the lid. Use an immersion blender to puree the soup until smooth.
6. Stir in the heavy cream and fresh basil. Season with salt and pepper to taste.
7. Serve hot, garnished with grated Parmesan cheese.

Nutritional Info: Calories: 250 | Fat: 14g | Carbs: 23g | Protein: 4g

Hearty Beef and Vegetable Stew

Prep: 15 mins | Cook: 40 mins | Serves: 6

Ingredients:

- US: 2 tablespoons olive oil, 1.5 pounds beef stew meat (cubed), 1 onion (chopped), 2 cloves garlic (minced), 3 carrots (sliced), 3 potatoes (diced), 2 cups beef broth, 1 cup red wine, 1 tablespoon tomato paste, 1 teaspoon thyme, 1 teaspoon rosemary, salt, pepper, 1 cup peas (frozen)
- UK: 2 tablespoons olive oil, 680g beef stew meat (cubed), 1 onion (chopped), 2 cloves garlic (minced), 3 carrots (sliced), 3 potatoes (diced), 480ml beef broth, 240ml red wine, 1 tablespoon tomato paste, 1 teaspoon thyme, 1 teaspoon rosemary, salt, pepper, 1 cup peas (frozen)

Instructions:

1. Set the Ninja Foodi to 'Sear/Sauté' on medium-high heat. Add the olive oil and brown the beef stew meat in batches. Remove and set aside.

2. Add the chopped onion and minced garlic to the pot, sautéing until softened.
3. Return the beef to the pot and add the sliced carrots, diced potatoes, beef broth, red wine, tomato paste, thyme, rosemary, salt, and pepper. Stir to combine.
4. Secure the pressure lid, set the vent to 'Seal,' and select 'Pressure Cook' on high for 30 minutes.
5. Quick release the pressure and remove the lid. Stir in the frozen peas and let them heat through for a few minutes.
6. Serve hot.

Nutritional Info: Calories: 350 | Fat: 14g | Carbs: 28g | Protein: 28g

Chicken Tortilla Soup

Prep: 10 mins | Cook: 20 mins | Serves: 4

Ingredients:
- US: 2 tablespoons olive oil, 1 onion (chopped), 2 cloves garlic (minced), 1 pound boneless, skinless chicken breasts (cubed), 1 can (14.5 oz) diced tomatoes, 1 can (4 oz) green chilies, 4 cups chicken broth, 1 teaspoon cumin, 1 teaspoon chili powder, 1/2 teaspoon paprika, salt, pepper, 1 cup corn (frozen), 1 cup black beans (rinsed and drained), tortilla chips, shredded cheese, chopped cilantro (for garnish)
- UK: 2 tablespoons olive oil, 1 onion (chopped), 2 cloves garlic (minced), 450g boneless, skinless chicken breasts (cubed), 1 can (400g) diced tomatoes, 1 can (113g) green chilies, 960ml chicken broth, 1 teaspoon cumin, 1 teaspoon chili powder, 1/2 teaspoon paprika, salt, pepper, 1 cup corn (frozen), 1 cup black beans (rinsed and drained), tortilla chips, shredded cheese, chopped cilantro (for garnish)

Instructions:
1. Set the Ninja Foodi to 'Sear/Sauté' on medium heat. Add the olive oil and sauté the chopped onion until soft and translucent, about 5 minutes.
2. Add the minced garlic and cook for another minute.
3. Add the cubed chicken and cook until browned on all sides.
4. Add the diced tomatoes, green chilies, chicken broth, cumin, chili powder, paprika, salt, and pepper. Stir to combine.
5. Secure the pressure lid, set the vent to 'Seal,' and select 'Pressure Cook' on high for 10 minutes.
6. Quick release the pressure and remove the lid. Stir in the frozen corn and black beans.
7. Serve hot, topped with tortilla chips, shredded cheese, and chopped cilantro.

Nutritional Info: Calories: 300 | Fat: 10g | Carbs: 28g | Protein: 28g

Butternut Squash and Apple Soup

Prep: 10 mins | Cook: 20 mins | Serves: 4

Ingredients:

- US: 2 tablespoons olive oil, 1 onion (chopped), 2 cloves garlic (minced), 1 large butternut squash (peeled, seeded, and cubed), 2 apples (peeled, cored, and chopped), 4 cups vegetable broth, 1 teaspoon ground cinnamon, 1/2 teaspoon ground nutmeg, salt, pepper, 1/2 cup heavy cream
- UK: 2 tablespoons olive oil, 1 onion (chopped), 2 cloves garlic (minced), 1 large butternut squash (peeled, seeded, and cubed), 2 apples (peeled, cored, and chopped), 960ml vegetable broth, 1 teaspoon ground cinnamon, 1/2 teaspoon ground nutmeg, salt, pepper, 120ml heavy cream

Instructions:

1. Set the Ninja Foodi to 'Sear/Sauté' on medium heat. Add the olive oil and sauté the chopped onion until soft and translucent, about 5 minutes.
2. Add the minced garlic and cook for another minute.
3. Add the cubed butternut squash, chopped apples, vegetable broth, ground cinnamon, ground nutmeg, salt, and pepper. Stir to combine.
4. Secure the pressure lid, set the vent to 'Seal,' and select 'Pressure Cook' on high for 10 minutes.
5. Quick release the pressure and remove the lid. Use an immersion blender to puree the soup until smooth.
6. Stir in the heavy cream. Serve hot.

Nutritional Info: Calories: 200 | Fat: 10g | Carbs: 28g | Protein: 2g

Lentil and Sausage Stew

Prep: 10 mins | Cook: 30 mins | Serves: 6

Ingredients:

- US: 1 tablespoon olive oil, 1 pound sausage (sliced), 1 onion (chopped), 2 carrots (sliced), 2 celery stalks (chopped), 2 cloves garlic (minced), 1 cup dried lentils (rinsed), 4 cups chicken broth, 1 can (14.5 oz) diced tomatoes, 1 teaspoon thyme, 1 teaspoon rosemary, salt, pepper
- UK: 1 tablespoon olive oil, 450g sausage (sliced), 1 onion (chopped), 2 carrots (sliced), 2 celery stalks (chopped), 2 cloves garlic (minced), 200g dried lentils (rinsed), 960ml chicken broth, 1 can (400g) diced tomatoes, 1 teaspoon thyme, 1 teaspoon rosemary, salt, pepper

Instructions:

1. Set the Ninja Foodi to 'Sear/Sauté' on medium-high heat. Add the olive oil and brown the sausage slices. Remove and set aside.
2. Add the chopped onion, sliced carrots, and chopped celery to the pot, sautéing until softened.
3. Add the minced garlic and cook for another minute.

4. Return the sausage to the pot and add the dried lentils, chicken broth, diced tomatoes, thyme, rosemary, salt, and pepper. Stir to combine.
5. Secure the pressure lid, set the vent to 'Seal,' and select 'Pressure Cook' on high for 20 minutes.
6. Quick release the pressure and remove the lid. Serve hot.

Nutritional Info: Calories: 320 | Fat: 12g | Carbs: 35g | Protein: 18g

Broccoli Cheddar Soup

Prep: 10 mins | Cook: 20 mins | Serves: 4

Ingredients:

- US: 2 tablespoons butter, 1 onion (chopped), 2 cloves garlic (minced), 4 cups broccoli florets, 2 cups chicken broth, 1 cup heavy cream, 2 cups shredded cheddar cheese, salt, pepper
- UK: 2 tablespoons butter, 1 onion (chopped), 2 cloves garlic (minced), 4 cups broccoli florets, 480ml chicken broth, 240ml heavy cream, 225g shredded cheddar cheese, salt, pepper

Instructions:

1. Set the Ninja Foodi to 'Sear/Sauté' on medium heat. Add the butter and sauté the chopped onion until soft and translucent, about 5 minutes.
2. Add the minced garlic and cook for another minute.
3. Add the broccoli florets and chicken broth. Stir to combine.
4. Secure the pressure lid, set the vent to 'Seal,' and select 'Pressure Cook' on high for 10 minutes.
5. Quick release the pressure and remove the lid. Use an immersion blender to puree the soup until smooth.
6. Stir in the heavy cream and shredded cheddar cheese until melted and well combined. Season with salt and pepper.
7. Serve hot.

Nutritional Info: Calories: 400 | Fat: 30g | Carbs: 15g | Protein: 18g

Minestrone Soup with Pesto

Prep: 15 mins | Cook: 30 mins | Serves: 6

Ingredients:

- US: 2 tablespoons olive oil, 1 onion (chopped), 2 cloves garlic (minced), 2 carrots (sliced), 2 celery stalks (chopped), 1 zucchini (chopped), 1 can (14.5 oz) diced tomatoes, 1 can (15 oz) cannellini beans (rinsed and drained), 4 cups vegetable broth, 1 cup pasta (small shape), 1 teaspoon thyme, 1 teaspoon oregano, salt, pepper, 1/4 cup pesto
- UK: 2 tablespoons olive oil, 1 onion (chopped), 2 cloves garlic (minced), 2 carrots (sliced), 2 celery stalks (chopped), 1 zucchini (chopped), 1 can (400g) diced tomatoes, 1 can (400g) cannellini beans (rinsed and drained), 960ml vegetable broth, 100g pasta (small shape), 1 teaspoon thyme, 1 teaspoon oregano, salt, pepper, 1/4 cup pesto

Instructions:

1. Set the Ninja Foodi to 'Sear/Sauté' on medium heat. Add the olive oil and sauté the chopped onion until soft and translucent, about 5 minutes.
2. Add the minced garlic, sliced carrots, chopped celery, and chopped zucchini. Cook for another 5 minutes.
3. Add the diced tomatoes, cannellini beans, vegetable broth, pasta, thyme, oregano, salt, and pepper. Stir to combine.
4. Secure the pressure lid, set the vent to 'Seal,' and select 'Pressure Cook' on high for 15 minutes.
5. Quick release the pressure and remove the lid. Stir in the pesto.
6. Serve hot.

Nutritional Info: Calories: 350 | Fat: 14g | Carbs: 45g | Protein: 12g

Loaded Baked Potato Soup

Prep: 10 mins | Cook: 20 mins | Serves: 4

Ingredients:

- US: 4 large russet potatoes (peeled and cubed), 1 onion (chopped), 2 cloves garlic (minced), 4 cups chicken broth, 1 cup heavy cream, 1 cup shredded cheddar cheese, 1/2 cup sour cream, 4 slices bacon (cooked and crumbled), salt, pepper, chopped chives (for garnish)
- UK: 4 large russet potatoes (peeled and cubed), 1 onion (chopped), 2 cloves garlic (minced), 960ml chicken broth, 240ml heavy cream, 225g shredded cheddar cheese, 120ml sour cream, 4 slices bacon (cooked and crumbled), salt, pepper, chopped chives (for garnish)

Instructions:

1. Set the Ninja Foodi to 'Sear/Sauté' on medium heat. Add the chopped onion and sauté until soft and translucent, about 5 minutes.
2. Add the minced garlic and cook for another minute.
3. Add the cubed potatoes and chicken broth. Stir to combine.
4. Secure the pressure lid, set the vent to 'Seal,' and select 'Pressure Cook' on high for 10 minutes.
5. Quick release the pressure and remove the lid. Use a potato masher or immersion blender to mash some of the potatoes for a thicker consistency.
6. Stir in the heavy cream, shredded cheddar cheese, and sour cream. Season with salt and pepper.
7. Serve hot, topped with crumbled bacon and chopped chives.

Nutritional Info: Calories: 450 | Fat: 25g | Carbs: 45g | Protein: 15g

Chili Con Carne

Prep: 15 mins | Cook: 40 mins | Serves: 6

Ingredients:

- US: 2 tablespoons olive oil, 1 onion (chopped), 2 cloves garlic (minced), 1 pound ground beef, 1 can (14.5 oz) diced tomatoes, 1 can (15 oz) kidney beans (rinsed and drained), 2 cups beef broth, 2 tablespoons chili powder, 1 teaspoon cumin, 1 teaspoon paprika, 1/2 teaspoon cayenne pepper, salt, pepper, shredded cheese (for garnish), sour cream (for garnish)
- UK: 2 tablespoons olive oil, 1 onion (chopped), 2 cloves garlic (minced), 450g ground beef, 1 can (400g) diced tomatoes, 1 can (400g) kidney beans (rinsed and drained), 480ml beef broth, 2 tablespoons chili powder, 1 teaspoon cumin, 1 teaspoon paprika, 1/2 teaspoon cayenne pepper, salt, pepper, shredded cheese (for garnish), sour cream (for garnish)

Instructions:

1. Set the Ninja Foodi to 'Sear/Sauté' on medium-high heat. Add the olive oil and sauté the chopped onion until soft and translucent, about 5 minutes.
2. Add the minced garlic and cook for another minute.
3. Add the ground beef and cook until browned. Drain any excess fat.
4. Add the diced tomatoes, kidney beans, beef broth, chili powder, cumin, paprika, cayenne pepper, salt, and pepper. Stir to combine.
5. Secure the pressure lid, set the vent to 'Seal,' and select 'Pressure Cook' on high for 20 minutes.
6. Quick release the pressure and remove the lid. Serve hot, topped with shredded cheese and sour cream.

Nutritional Info: Calories: 400 | Fat: 20g | Carbs: 30g | Protein: 25g

Thai Coconut Curry Soup

Prep: 10 mins | Cook: 20 mins | Serves: 4

Ingredients:

- US: 2 tablespoons coconut oil, 1 onion (chopped), 2 cloves garlic (minced), 1 tablespoon ginger (minced), 1 pound chicken breast (cubed), 2 cups chicken broth, 1 can (14 oz) coconut milk, 2 tablespoons red curry paste, 1 tablespoon fish sauce, 1 red bell pepper (sliced), 1 cup mushrooms (sliced), 1 cup snow peas, 1 lime (juiced), fresh cilantro (for garnish)
- UK: 2 tablespoons coconut oil, 1 onion (chopped), 2 cloves garlic (minced), 1 tablespoon ginger (minced), 450g chicken breast (cubed), 480ml chicken broth, 1 can (400ml) coconut milk, 2 tablespoons red curry paste, 1 tablespoon fish sauce, 1 red bell pepper (sliced), 1 cup mushrooms (sliced), 1 cup snow peas, 1 lime (juiced), fresh cilantro (for garnish)

Instructions:

1. Set the Ninja Foodi to 'Sear/Sauté' on medium heat. Add the coconut oil and sauté the chopped onion, minced garlic, and minced ginger until fragrant, about 5 minutes.
2. Add the cubed chicken breast and cook until browned.

3. Add the chicken broth, coconut milk, red curry paste, fish sauce, sliced red bell pepper, sliced mushrooms, and snow peas. Stir to combine.
4. Secure the pressure lid, set the vent to 'Seal,' and select 'Pressure Cook' on high for 10 minutes.
5. Quick release the pressure and remove the lid. Stir in the lime juice.
6. Serve hot, garnished with fresh cilantro.

Nutritional Info: Calories: 350 | Fat: 20g | Carbs: 20g | Protein: 25g

Vegetable Lasagna with Ricotta and Spinach

Prep: 15 mins | Cook: 1 hour | Serves: 6

Ingredients:

- US: 300g lasagna noodles, 500g ricotta cheese, 300g fresh spinach, 700g marinara sauce, 2 cups shredded mozzarella cheese, 1/2 cup grated Parmesan cheese, 1 egg, 2 cloves garlic (minced), 1 tablespoon olive oil, salt, pepper
- UK: 300g lasagna noodles, 500g ricotta cheese, 300g fresh spinach, 700g marinara sauce, 200g shredded mozzarella cheese, 50g grated Parmesan cheese, 1 egg, 2 cloves garlic (minced), 1 tablespoon olive oil, salt, pepper

Instructions:

1. Preheat the Ninja Foodi using the BAKE/ROAST function at 350°F (175°C).
2. Cook lasagna noodles according to package instructions. Drain and set aside.
3. In a large skillet, heat olive oil over medium heat. Add minced garlic and sauté until fragrant.
4. Add spinach to the skillet and cook until wilted. Remove from heat and let cool.
5. In a mixing bowl, combine ricotta cheese, egg, salt, and pepper. Stir in the cooked spinach.
6. Spread a thin layer of marinara sauce on the bottom of the Ninja Foodi pot.
7. Layer lasagna noodles, ricotta mixture, marinara sauce, and mozzarella cheese. Repeat until all ingredients are used, ending with a layer of mozzarella and Parmesan cheese on top.
8. Close the lid and select the BAKE/ROAST function. Set the temperature to 350°F (175°C) and cook for 40 minutes.
9. Let the lasagna cool for 10 minutes before serving.

Nutritional Info: Calories: 450 | Fat: 18g | Carbs: 50g | Protein: 22g

Quinoa and Black Bean Burgers

Prep: 20 mins | Cook: 15 mins | Serves: 4

Ingredients:

- US: 1 cup quinoa, 1 can black beans (drained and rinsed), 1 red bell pepper (finely chopped), 1 small red onion (finely chopped), 2 cloves garlic (minced), 1 teaspoon cumin, 1 teaspoon smoked paprika, 1/2 cup breadcrumbs, 1 egg, salt, pepper, olive oil for frying
- UK: 200g quinoa, 1 can black beans (drained and rinsed), 1 red bell pepper (finely chopped), 1 small red onion (finely chopped), 2 cloves garlic (minced), 1 teaspoon cumin, 1 teaspoon smoked paprika, 50g breadcrumbs, 1 egg, salt, pepper, olive oil for frying

Instructions:

1. Cook quinoa according to package instructions and let cool.
2. In a large mixing bowl, mash black beans with a fork until mostly smooth.

3. Add cooked quinoa, chopped bell pepper, red onion, garlic, cumin, smoked paprika, breadcrumbs, egg, salt, and pepper. Mix until well combined.
4. Form the mixture into 4 patties.
5. Preheat the Ninja Foodi using the AIR CRISP function at 375°F (190°C).
6. Brush the patties lightly with olive oil and place them in the Ninja Foodi basket.
7. Air crisp the patties for 15 minutes, flipping halfway through, until golden and crispy.
8. Serve on buns with your favorite toppings.

Nutritional Info: Calories: 320 | Fat: 10g | Carbs: 45g | Protein: 12g

Vegetarian Chili with Sweet Potatoes

Prep: 15 mins | Cook: 45 mins | Serves: 6

Ingredients:
- US: 1 large sweet potato (peeled and cubed), 1 can black beans (drained and rinsed), 1 can kidney beans (drained and rinsed), 1 can diced tomatoes, 1 bell pepper (chopped), 1 onion (chopped), 2 cloves garlic (minced), 2 tablespoons chili powder, 1 teaspoon cumin, 1 teaspoon smoked paprika, 4 cups vegetable broth, salt, pepper, avocado (for garnish), cilantro (for garnish)
- UK: 1 large sweet potato (peeled and cubed), 1 can black beans (drained and rinsed), 1 can kidney beans (drained and rinsed), 1 can chopped tomatoes, 1 bell pepper (chopped), 1 onion (chopped), 2 cloves garlic (minced), 2 tablespoons chili powder, 1 teaspoon cumin, 1 teaspoon smoked paprika, 1 liter vegetable stock, salt, pepper, avocado (for garnish), coriander (for garnish)

Instructions:
1. Preheat the Ninja Foodi using the SAUTÉ function.
2. Add chopped onion and garlic to the pot and sauté until soft.
3. Add sweet potatoes, bell pepper, chili powder, cumin, and smoked paprika. Cook for 5 minutes, stirring occasionally.
4. Add black beans, kidney beans, diced tomatoes, and vegetable broth. Stir to combine.
5. Close the lid and set the Ninja Foodi to PRESSURE COOK on high for 10 minutes.
6. Once the cooking cycle is complete, perform a quick release of the pressure.
7. Open the lid and stir the chili. Adjust seasoning with salt and pepper to taste.
8. Serve with avocado slices and cilantro garnish.

Nutritional Info: Calories: 300 | Fat: 6g | Carbs: 55g | Protein: 12g

Falafel Bowls with Tahini Sauce

Prep: 20 mins | Cook: 15 mins | Serves: 4

Ingredients:
- US: 2 cans chickpeas (drained and rinsed), 1 small onion (chopped), 3 cloves garlic, 1/4 cup fresh parsley, 2 tablespoons flour, 1 teaspoon cumin, 1 teaspoon coriander, 1/2 teaspoon baking powder, salt, pepper, olive oil for frying, 1 cup quinoa (cooked), 1 cucumber (diced), 1 tomato (diced), 1/4 cup tahini, 2 tablespoons lemon juice, water (as needed)
- UK: 2 cans chickpeas (drained and rinsed), 1 small onion (chopped), 3 cloves garlic, 1/4 cup fresh parsley, 2 tablespoons flour, 1 teaspoon cumin, 1 teaspoon coriander, 1/2 teaspoon baking powder, salt, pepper, olive oil for frying, 200g quinoa (cooked), 1 cucumber (diced), 1 tomato (diced), 60ml tahini, 2 tablespoons lemon juice, water (as needed)

Instructions:
1. In a food processor, combine chickpeas, onion, garlic, parsley, flour, cumin, coriander, baking powder, salt, and pepper. Process until smooth.
2. Form the mixture into small balls or patties.
3. Preheat the Ninja Foodi using the AIR CRISP function at 375°F (190°C).
4. Lightly brush the falafel with olive oil and place in the Ninja Foodi basket.
5. Air crisp for 15 minutes, turning halfway through, until crispy and golden.
6. In a small bowl, mix tahini and lemon juice. Add water a little at a time until you reach a pourable consistency.
7. Assemble bowls with cooked quinoa, diced cucumber, diced tomato, and falafel. Drizzle with tahini sauce.

Nutritional Info: Calories: 350 | Fat: 15g | Carbs: 45g | Protein: 12g

Stuffed Portobello Mushrooms with Feta

Prep: 15 mins | Cook: 20 mins | Serves: 4

Ingredients:
- US: 4 large portobello mushrooms, 1 cup cooked quinoa, 1/2 cup crumbled feta cheese, 1 small red bell pepper (chopped), 2 green onions (chopped), 2 cloves garlic (minced), 2 tablespoons olive oil, salt, pepper, fresh parsley (for garnish)
- UK: 4 large portobello mushrooms, 200g cooked quinoa, 50g crumbled feta cheese, 1 small red bell pepper (chopped), 2 spring onions (chopped), 2 cloves garlic (minced), 2 tablespoons olive oil, salt, pepper, fresh parsley (for garnish)

Instructions:
1. Preheat the Ninja Foodi using the BAKE/ROAST function at 375°F (190°C).
2. Remove the stems from the portobello mushrooms and brush the caps with olive oil. Season with salt and pepper.

3. In a mixing bowl, combine cooked quinoa, feta cheese, bell pepper, green onions, and garlic. Mix well.
4. Stuff the mushroom caps with the quinoa mixture.
5. Place the stuffed mushrooms in the Ninja Foodi pot.
6. Close the lid and set to BAKE/ROAST at 375°F (190°C) for 20 minutes.
7. Garnish with fresh parsley before serving.

Nutritional Info: Calories: 250 | Fat: 12g | Carbs: 25g | Protein: 10g

Vegetable Stir-Fry with Tofu

Prep: 10 mins | Cook: 15 mins | Serves: 4

Ingredients:

- US: 1 block firm tofu (pressed and cubed), 2 tablespoons soy sauce, 1 tablespoon sesame oil, 2 cups broccoli florets, 1 red bell pepper (sliced), 1 yellow bell pepper (sliced), 1 carrot (sliced), 1 small onion (sliced), 2 cloves garlic (minced), 1 teaspoon ginger (grated), 2 tablespoons vegetable oil, sesame seeds (for garnish), green onions (sliced for garnish)
- UK: 1 block firm tofu (pressed and cubed), 2 tablespoons soy sauce, 1 tablespoon sesame oil, 2 cups broccoli florets, 1 red bell pepper (sliced), 1 yellow bell pepper (sliced), 1 carrot (sliced), 1 small onion (sliced), 2 cloves garlic (minced), 1 teaspoon ginger (grated), 2 tablespoons vegetable oil, sesame seeds (for garnish), spring onions (sliced for garnish)

Instructions:

1. In a small bowl, mix tofu cubes with soy sauce and sesame oil. Let marinate for 10 minutes.
2. Preheat the Ninja Foodi using the SAUTÉ function.
3. Add vegetable oil to the pot and heat until shimmering.
4. Add marinated tofu and cook until golden brown on all sides. Remove from the pot and set aside.
5. Add garlic and ginger to the pot and sauté until fragrant.
6. Add broccoli, bell peppers, carrot, and onion. Stir-fry for 57 minutes until vegetables are tender-crisp.
7. Return tofu to the pot and toss to combine.
8. Garnish with sesame seeds and green onions before serving.

Nutritional Info: Calories: 300 | Fat: 18g | Carbs: 20g | Protein: 15g

Lentil and Sweet Potato Shepherd's Pie

Prep: 20 mins | Cook: 30 mins | Serves: 6
Ingredients:

- US: 2 large sweet potatoes (peeled and cubed), 1 cup green lentils, 1 onion (chopped), 2 cloves garlic (minced), 2 carrots (chopped), 1 cup frozen peas, 2 cups vegetable broth, 2 tablespoons tomato paste, 1 teaspoon thyme, 1 teaspoon rosemary, salt, pepper, 2 tablespoons olive oil
- UK: 2 large sweet potatoes (peeled and cubed), 200g green lentils, 1 onion (chopped), 2 cloves garlic (minced), 2 carrots (chopped), 1 cup frozen peas, 500ml vegetable stock, 2 tablespoons tomato purée, 1 teaspoon thyme, 1 teaspoon rosemary, salt, pepper, 2 tablespoons olive oil

Instructions:

1. Preheat the Ninja Foodi using the SAUTÉ function.
2. Add olive oil, chopped onion, and garlic to the pot. Sauté until soft.
3. Add chopped carrots, green lentils, tomato paste, thyme, rosemary, and vegetable broth. Stir to combine.
4. Close the lid and set to PRESSURE COOK on high for 15 minutes.
5. Meanwhile, boil sweet potatoes until tender. Drain and mash with salt and pepper.
6. Once the pressure cooking cycle is complete, perform a quick release.
7. Stir in frozen peas into the lentil mixture.
8. Spread the lentil mixture in an even layer and top with mashed sweet potatoes.
9. Set the Ninja Foodi to BAKE/ROAST at 375°F (190°C) for 10 minutes to brown the top.
10. Let cool slightly before serving.

Nutritional Info: Calories: 350 | Fat: 8g | Carbs: 60g | Protein: 12g

Cauliflower Steaks with Chimichurri

Prep: 15 mins | Cook: 20 mins | Serves: 4
Ingredients:

- US: 1 large cauliflower (cut into steaks), 1/4 cup olive oil, 2 tablespoons lemon juice, 2 cloves garlic (minced), salt, pepper, 1 cup fresh parsley, 1/2 cup fresh cilantro, 1/4 cup red wine vinegar, 1/2 teaspoon red pepper flakes
- UK: 1 large cauliflower (cut into steaks), 60ml olive oil, 2 tablespoons lemon juice, 2 cloves garlic (minced), salt, pepper, 1 cup fresh parsley, 1/2 cup fresh coriander, 60ml red wine vinegar, 1/2 teaspoon red pepper flakes

Instructions:

1. Preheat the Ninja Foodi using the BAKE/ROAST function at 400°F (200°C).
2. Brush cauliflower steaks with olive oil and season with salt and pepper.
3. Place cauliflower steaks in the Ninja Foodi pot.

4. Close the lid and set to BAKE/ROAST at 400°F (200°C) for 20 minutes, flipping halfway through.
5. Meanwhile, make the chimichurri sauce by blending parsley, cilantro, red wine vinegar, garlic, lemon juice, red pepper flakes, salt, and remaining olive oil until smooth.
6. Once the cauliflower steaks are tender and golden, remove from the pot.
7. Drizzle with chimichurri sauce before serving.

Nutritional Info: Calories: 220 | Fat: 18g | Carbs: 15g | Protein: 4g

Vegetable Curry with Coconut Milk

Prep: 15 mins | Cook: 20 mins | Serves: 4

Ingredients:

- US: 1 tablespoon coconut oil, 1 onion (chopped), 3 cloves garlic (minced), 1 tablespoon ginger (grated), 1 tablespoon curry powder, 1 teaspoon turmeric, 1 teaspoon cumin, 1 can coconut milk, 1 cup vegetable broth, 2 cups cauliflower florets, 1 bell pepper (sliced), 1 cup green beans (trimmed), 1 cup chickpeas (drained and rinsed), salt, pepper, fresh cilantro (for garnish)
- UK: 1 tablespoon coconut oil, 1 onion (chopped), 3 cloves garlic (minced), 1 tablespoon ginger (grated), 1 tablespoon curry powder, 1 teaspoon turmeric, 1 teaspoon cumin, 1 can coconut milk, 250ml vegetable stock, 2 cups cauliflower florets, 1 bell pepper (sliced), 1 cup green beans (trimmed), 1 cup chickpeas (drained and rinsed), salt, pepper, fresh coriander (for garnish)

Instructions:

1. Preheat the Ninja Foodi using the SAUTÉ function.
2. Add coconut oil to the pot and heat until melted.
3. Add chopped onion, garlic, and ginger. Sauté until fragrant.
4. Stir in curry powder, turmeric, and cumin. Cook for 1 minute.
5. Add cauliflower, bell pepper, green beans, chickpeas, coconut milk, and vegetable broth. Stir to combine.
6. Close the lid and set the Ninja Foodi to PRESSURE COOK on high for 5 minutes.
7. Once the cooking cycle is complete, perform a quick release of the pressure.
8. Open the lid and stir the curry. Adjust seasoning with salt and pepper to taste.
9. Garnish with fresh cilantro before serving.

Nutritional Info: Calories: 320 | Fat: 20g | Carbs: 30g | Protein: 8g

Prep: 15 mins | Cook: 20 mins | Serves: 4

Ingredients:

- US: 4 large bell peppers (tops cut off and seeds removed), 1 cup cooked quinoa, 1 can chickpeas (drained and rinsed), 1/2 cup crumbled feta cheese, 1/2 cup diced tomatoes, 1/4 cup chopped olives, 1 small red onion (chopped), 2 cloves garlic (minced), 2 tablespoons olive oil, 1 teaspoon oregano, salt, pepper, fresh basil (for garnish)
- UK: 4 large bell peppers (tops cut off and seeds removed), 200g cooked quinoa, 1 can chickpeas (drained and rinsed), 50g crumbled feta cheese, 1/2 cup diced tomatoes, 1/4 cup chopped olives, 1 small red onion (chopped), 2 cloves garlic (minced), 2 tablespoons olive oil, 1 teaspoon oregano, salt, pepper, fresh basil (for garnish)

Instructions:

1. Preheat the Ninja Foodi using the BAKE/ROAST function at 375°F (190°C).
2. In a large mixing bowl, combine cooked quinoa, chickpeas, feta cheese, diced tomatoes, chopped olives, red onion, garlic, olive oil, oregano, salt, and pepper. Mix well.
3. Stuff the bell peppers with the quinoa mixture.
4. Place the stuffed peppers in the Ninja Foodi pot.
5. Close the lid and set to BAKE/ROAST at 375°F (190°C) for 20 minutes.
6. Garnish with fresh basil before serving.

Nutritional Info: Calories: 290 | Fat: 12g | Carbs: 35g | Protein: 10g

CHAPTER 5: POULTRY AND MEAT MAINS

Juicy Chicken Breasts with Lemon Garlic Sauce

Prep: 10 mins | Cook: 25 mins | Serves: 4

Ingredients:

- US: 4 boneless, skinless chicken breasts, 2 tablespoons olive oil, 4 cloves garlic (minced), 1 lemon (juiced and zested), 1 cup chicken broth, 1 teaspoon dried thyme, salt, pepper, fresh parsley (for garnish)
- UK: 4 boneless, skinless chicken breasts, 2 tablespoons olive oil, 4 cloves garlic (minced), 1 lemon (juiced and zested), 250ml chicken stock, 1 teaspoon dried thyme, salt, pepper, fresh parsley (for garnish)

Instructions:

1. Preheat the Ninja Foodi using the SAUTÉ function.
2. Season chicken breasts with salt and pepper.
3. Add olive oil to the pot. Once hot, add chicken breasts and sear on each side until golden brown, about 4 minutes per side. Remove and set aside.
4. Add garlic to the pot and sauté until fragrant, about 1 minute.
5. Pour in chicken broth, lemon juice, lemon zest, and dried thyme. Stir to combine.
6. Return chicken breasts to the pot.
7. Close the lid and set to PRESSURE COOK on high for 8 minutes.
8. Once the cooking cycle is complete, perform a quick release of the pressure.
9. Remove chicken breasts and let rest for a few minutes.
10. Switch to the SAUTÉ function and let the sauce simmer until slightly thickened.
11. Serve chicken breasts with the lemon garlic sauce drizzled over and garnish with fresh parsley.

Nutritional Info: Calories: 300 | Fat: 12g | Carbs: 5g | Protein: 45g

Beef Brisket with Barbecue Sauce

Prep: 15 mins | Cook: 3 hours | Serves: 6

Ingredients:

- US: 2 lb beef brisket, 2 tablespoons olive oil, 1 onion (sliced), 3 cloves garlic (minced), 1 cup beef broth, 1 cup barbecue sauce, 1 teaspoon smoked paprika, 1 teaspoon chili powder, salt, pepper
- UK: 1 kg beef brisket, 2 tablespoons olive oil, 1 onion (sliced), 3 cloves garlic (minced), 250ml beef stock, 250ml barbecue sauce, 1 teaspoon smoked paprika, 1 teaspoon chili powder, salt, pepper

Instructions:

1. Preheat the Ninja Foodi using the SAUTÉ function.
2. Season the brisket with salt, pepper, smoked paprika, and chili powder.
3. Add olive oil to the pot. Once hot, sear the brisket on all sides until browned. Remove and set aside.
4. Add sliced onion and garlic to the pot, sauté until soft.
5. Pour in beef broth and stir to deglaze the pot.
6. Return the brisket to the pot and pour barbecue sauce over it.
7. Close the lid and set to PRESSURE COOK on high for 1.5 hours.
8. Once the cooking cycle is complete, allow for natural pressure release for 15 minutes, then perform a quick release.
9. Remove the brisket and let rest before slicing.
10. Use the SAUTÉ function to simmer the sauce until thickened.
11. Serve sliced brisket with the barbecue sauce.

Nutritional Info: Calories: 450 | Fat: 25g | Carbs: 20g | Protein: 35g

Turkey and Veggie Meatballs in Marinara

Prep: 15 mins | Cook: 25 mins | Serves: 4

Ingredients:

- US: 1 lb ground turkey, 1/2 cup breadcrumbs, 1 egg, 1 small zucchini (grated), 1 carrot (grated), 2 cloves garlic (minced), 1/4 cup Parmesan cheese (grated), 1 teaspoon Italian seasoning, 2 cups marinara sauce, salt, pepper, olive oil for browning
- UK: 500g ground turkey, 50g breadcrumbs, 1 egg, 1 small courgette (grated), 1 carrot (grated), 2 cloves garlic (minced), 25g Parmesan cheese (grated), 1 teaspoon Italian seasoning, 500ml marinara sauce, salt, pepper, olive oil for browning

Instructions:

1. In a large bowl, mix ground turkey, breadcrumbs, egg, grated zucchini, grated carrot, minced garlic, Parmesan cheese, Italian seasoning, salt, and pepper.
2. Form the mixture into meatballs.
3. Preheat the Ninja Foodi using the SAUTÉ function.

4. Add olive oil to the pot. Once hot, brown the meatballs on all sides. Remove and set aside.
5. Add marinara sauce to the pot and deglaze.
6. Return the meatballs to the pot.
7. Close the lid and set to PRESSURE COOK on high for 10 minutes.
8. Once the cooking cycle is complete, perform a quick release of the pressure.
9. Serve meatballs with marinara sauce.

Nutritional Info: Calories: 320 | Fat: 15g | Carbs: 18g | Protein: 30g

Honey Garlic Pork Chops

Prep: 10 mins | Cook: 20 mins | Serves: 4

Ingredients:

- US: 4 pork chops, 2 tablespoons olive oil, 3 cloves garlic (minced), 1/4 cup honey, 1/4 cup soy sauce, 1/4 cup chicken broth, 1 tablespoon apple cider vinegar, salt, pepper, chopped green onions (for garnish)
- UK: 4 pork chops, 2 tablespoons olive oil, 3 cloves garlic (minced), 60ml honey, 60ml soy sauce, 60ml chicken stock, 1 tablespoon apple cider vinegar, salt, pepper, chopped spring onions (for garnish)

Instructions:

1. Preheat the Ninja Foodi using the SAUTÉ function.
2. Season pork chops with salt and pepper.
3. Add olive oil to the pot. Once hot, sear pork chops on both sides until golden brown. Remove and set aside.
4. Add garlic to the pot and sauté until fragrant.
5. Stir in honey, soy sauce, chicken broth, and apple cider vinegar.
6. Return pork chops to the pot.
7. Close the lid and set to PRESSURE COOK on high for 8 minutes.
8. Once the cooking cycle is complete, perform a quick release of the pressure.
9. Serve pork chops with the honey garlic sauce and garnish with chopped green onions.

Nutritional Info: Calories: 400 | Fat: 20g | Carbs: 25g | Protein: 30g

Beef and Broccoli Stir-Fry

Prep: 15 mins | Cook: 20 mins | Serves: 4

Ingredients:

- US: 1 lb flank steak (sliced thinly), 2 tablespoons soy sauce, 2 tablespoons oyster sauce, 1 tablespoon cornstarch, 2 cups broccoli florets, 1 bell pepper (sliced), 1 onion (sliced), 2 cloves garlic (minced), 1 tablespoon sesame oil, 1/4 cup beef broth, 1 teaspoon ginger (grated), sesame seeds (for garnish)
- UK: 500g flank steak (sliced thinly), 2 tablespoons soy sauce, 2 tablespoons oyster sauce, 1 tablespoon cornstarch, 2 cups broccoli florets, 1 bell pepper (sliced), 1 onion (sliced), 2 cloves garlic (minced), 1 tablespoon sesame oil, 60ml beef stock, 1 teaspoon ginger (grated), sesame seeds (for garnish)

Instructions:

1. In a bowl, mix sliced beef with soy sauce, oyster sauce, and cornstarch. Let marinate for 10 minutes.
2. Preheat the Ninja Foodi using the SAUTÉ function.
3. Add sesame oil to the pot. Once hot, add garlic and ginger, sauté until fragrant.
4. Add marinated beef and cook until browned. Remove and set aside.
5. Add broccoli, bell pepper, and onion to the pot. Stirfry until tendercrisp.
6. Return beef to the pot and stir in beef broth.
7. Close the lid and set to PRESSURE COOK on high for 3 minutes.
8. Once the cooking cycle is complete, perform a quick release of the pressure.
9. Serve with sesame seeds garnish.

Nutritional Info: Calories: 350 | Fat: 20g | Carbs: 15g | Protein: 30g

Chicken Fajitas with Peppers and Onions

Prep: 10 mins | Cook: 15 mins | Serves: 4

Ingredients:

- US: 1 lb chicken breast (sliced), 1 red bell pepper (sliced), 1 green bell pepper (sliced), 1 onion (sliced), 2 tablespoons olive oil, 1 tablespoon fajita seasoning, 1 lime (juiced), salt, pepper, tortillas, chopped cilantro (for garnish)
- UK: 500g chicken breast (sliced), 1 red bell pepper (sliced), 1 green bell pepper (sliced), 1 onion (sliced), 2 tablespoons olive oil, 1 tablespoon fajita seasoning, 1 lime (juiced), salt, pepper, tortillas, chopped coriander (for garnish)

Instructions:

1. Preheat the Ninja Foodi using the SAUTÉ function.
2. Season sliced chicken with fajita seasoning, salt, and pepper.
3. Add olive oil to the pot. Once hot, add chicken and cook until browned.
4. Add bell peppers and onion. Cook until tender.

5. Squeeze lime juice over the mixture and stir to combine.
6. Serve in tortillas and garnish with chopped cilantro.

Nutritional Info: Calories: 400 | Fat: 15g | Carbs: 35g | Protein: 30g

Meatloaf with Mashed Potatoes

Prep: 20 mins | Cook: 1 hour | Serves: 4

Ingredients:

- US: 1 lb ground beef, 1/2 cup breadcrumbs, 1 egg, 1 onion (finely chopped), 2 cloves garlic (minced), 1/4 cup ketchup, 1 tablespoon Worcestershire sauce, 2 lbs potatoes (peeled and cubed), 1/2 cup milk, 2 tablespoons butter, salt, pepper
- UK: 500g ground beef, 50g breadcrumbs, 1 egg, 1 onion (finely chopped), 2 cloves garlic (minced), 60ml ketchup, 1 tablespoon Worcestershire sauce, 1 kg potatoes (peeled and cubed), 120ml milk, 2 tablespoons butter, salt, pepper

Instructions:

1. In a large bowl, mix ground beef, breadcrumbs, egg, chopped onion, minced garlic, ketchup, Worcestershire sauce, salt, and pepper.
2. Shape the mixture into a loaf and place it in the Ninja Foodi pot.
3. Close the lid and set to BAKE/ROAST at 350°F (175°C) for 45 minutes.
4. Meanwhile, boil potatoes until tender. Drain and mash with milk, butter, salt, and pepper.
5. Once the meatloaf is done, let it rest for a few minutes before slicing.
6. Serve meatloaf with mashed potatoes.

Nutritional Info: Calories: 600 | Fat: 30g | Carbs: 50g | Protein: 30g

Teriyaki Chicken Thighs

Prep: 10 mins | Cook: 25 mins | Serves: 4

Ingredients:

- US: 8 chicken thighs (boneless, skinless), 1/4 cup soy sauce, 1/4 cup mirin, 1/4 cup honey, 2 tablespoons rice vinegar, 2 cloves garlic (minced), 1 teaspoon ginger (grated), 1 tablespoon cornstarch, 1/4 cup water, sesame seeds (for garnish), sliced green onions (for garnish)
- UK: 8 chicken thighs (boneless, skinless), 60ml soy sauce, 60ml mirin, 60ml honey, 2 tablespoons rice vinegar, 2 cloves garlic (minced), 1 teaspoon ginger (grated), 1 tablespoon cornstarch, 60ml water, sesame seeds (for garnish), sliced spring onions (for garnish)

Instructions:

1. Preheat the Ninja Foodi using the SAUTÉ function.
2. In a bowl, mix soy sauce, mirin, honey, rice vinegar, minced garlic, and grated ginger.
3. Add chicken thighs to the pot and brown on both sides.
4. Pour the sauce over the chicken thighs.
5. Close the lid and set to PRESSURE COOK on high for 15 minutes.
6. Once the cooking cycle is complete, perform a quick release of the pressure.
7. Remove the chicken thighs and set aside.

8. Mix cornstarch with water and add to the pot. Use the SAUTÉ function to simmer and thicken the sauce.
9. Serve chicken thighs with teriyaki sauce, garnished with sesame seeds and green onions.

Nutritional Info:M Calories: 450 | Fat: 20g | Carbs: 30g | Protein: 35g

Sausage and Pepperoni Pizza Pasta

Prep: 10 mins | Cook: 20 mins | Serves: 4

Ingredients:

- US: 1 lb Italian sausage (sliced), 1 cup pepperoni slices, 1 onion (chopped), 2 cloves garlic (minced), 1 bell pepper (sliced), 2 cups marinara sauce, 1 cup mozzarella cheese (shredded), 1/2 cup Parmesan cheese (grated), 2 cups pasta (uncooked), 2 cups water, salt, pepper, Italian seasoning
- UK: 500g Italian sausage (sliced), 1 cup pepperoni slices, 1 onion (chopped), 2 cloves garlic (minced), 1 bell pepper (sliced), 500ml marinara sauce, 1 cup mozzarella cheese (shredded), 50g Parmesan cheese (grated), 200g pasta (uncooked), 500ml water, salt, pepper, Italian seasoning

Instructions:

1. Preheat the Ninja Foodi using the SAUTÉ function.
2. Add sausage slices and cook until browned.
3. Add chopped onion, minced garlic, and bell pepper. Sauté until soft.
4. Add pasta, marinara sauce, water, salt, pepper, and Italian seasoning. Stir to combine.
5. Close the lid and set to PRESSURE COOK on high for 8 minutes.
6. Once the cooking cycle is complete, perform a quick release of the pressure.
7. Stir in pepperoni slices and top with mozzarella and Parmesan cheese.
8. Set the Ninja Foodi to BAKE/ROAST at 375°F (190°C) for 5 minutes to melt the cheese.
9. Serve hot.

Nutritional Info: Calories: 600 | Fat: 35g | Carbs: 45g | Protein: 25g

Mongolian Beef with Steamed Rice

Prep: 10 mins | Cook: 25 mins | Serves: 4

Ingredients:

- US: 1 lb flank steak (sliced thinly), 1/4 cup cornstarch, 2 tablespoons vegetable oil, 3 cloves garlic (minced), 1/4 cup soy sauce, 1/4 cup brown sugar, 1/4 cup water, 1 teaspoon ginger (grated), 2 cups broccoli florets, 2 cups cooked rice, sliced green onions (for garnish)
- UK: 500g flank steak (sliced thinly), 1/4 cup cornstarch, 2 tablespoons vegetable oil, 3 cloves garlic (minced), 60ml soy sauce, 60ml brown sugar, 60ml water, 1 teaspoon ginger (grated), 2 cups broccoli florets, 2 cups cooked rice, sliced spring onions (for garnish)

Instructions:

1. Toss sliced flank steak with cornstarch until evenly coated.
2. Preheat the Ninja Foodi using the SAUTÉ function.

3. Add vegetable oil to the pot. Once hot, add the steak and cook until browned. Remove and set aside.
4. Add garlic and ginger to the pot, sauté until fragrant.
5. Stir in soy sauce, brown sugar, and water. Cook until the sauce starts to thicken.
6. Return the beef to the pot and add broccoli florets.
7. Close the lid and set to PRESSURE COOK on high for 3 minutes.
8. Once the cooking cycle is complete, perform a quick release of the pressure.
9. Serve beef and broccoli over steamed rice, garnished with sliced green onions.

Nutritional Info: Calories: 500 | Fat: 20g | Carbs: 50g | Protein: 30g

Garlic Butter Shrimp Scampi

Prep: 10 mins | Cook: 15 mins | Serves: 4

Ingredients:

- US: 1 lb large shrimp (peeled and deveined), 4 tablespoons butter, 4 cloves garlic (minced), 1/4 cup white wine, 1 lemon (juiced), 1/4 cup fresh parsley (chopped), salt, pepper, cooked pasta (for serving)
- UK: 500g large shrimp (peeled and deveined), 60g butter, 4 cloves garlic (minced), 60ml white wine, 1 lemon (juiced), 60ml fresh parsley (chopped), salt, pepper, cooked pasta (for serving)

Instructions:

1. Preheat the Ninja Foodi using the SAUTÉ function.
2. Add butter to the pot and let it melt.
3. Add minced garlic and sauté until fragrant.
4. Pour in white wine and lemon juice, then let it simmer for a minute.
5. Add shrimp to the pot and cook until pink and opaque, about 34 minutes.
6. Season with salt, pepper, and stir in chopped parsley.
7. Serve shrimp scampi over cooked pasta.

Nutritional Info: Calories: 350 | Fat: 18g | Carbs: 10g | Protein: 30g

Salmon with Lemon Dill Sauce

Prep: 10 mins | Cook: 20 mins | Serves: 4

Ingredients:

- US: 4 salmon fillets, 2 tablespoons olive oil, 1 lemon (zested and juiced), 1/4 cup sour cream, 2 tablespoons fresh dill (chopped), salt, pepper
- UK: 4 salmon fillets, 30ml olive oil, 1 lemon (zested and juiced), 60ml sour cream, 2 tablespoons fresh dill (chopped), salt, pepper

Instructions:

1. Preheat the Ninja Foodi using the BAKE/ROAST function at 375°F (190°C).
2. Season salmon fillets with salt, pepper, and lemon zest.
3. Place salmon fillets on the rack inside the pot.
4. Bake/roast for 1520 minutes, until salmon is cooked through.
5. In a small bowl, mix sour cream, lemon juice, and chopped dill.
6. Serve salmon with the lemon dill sauce.

Nutritional Info: Calories: 400 | Fat: 25g | Carbs: 2g | Protein: 38g

Crispy Fish Tacos with Cabbage Slaw

Prep: 15 mins | Cook: 15 mins | Serves: 4

Ingredients:

- US: 1 lb white fish fillets (cut into strips), 1/2 cup flour, 1/2 cup cornmeal, 2 eggs (beaten), 2 cups shredded cabbage, 1/4 cup mayonnaise, 1 lime (juiced), 1 tablespoon cilantro (chopped), salt, pepper, tortillas, olive oil spray
- UK: 500g white fish fillets (cut into strips), 60g flour, 60g cornmeal, 2 eggs (beaten), 200g shredded cabbage, 60ml mayonnaise, 1 lime (juiced), 1 tablespoon cilantro (chopped), salt, pepper, tortillas, olive oil spray

Instructions:

1. Preheat the Ninja Foodi using the AIR CRISP function at 400°F (200°C).
2. Set up a breading station with flour, beaten eggs, and cornmeal.
3. Coat fish strips in flour, dip in eggs, then coat with cornmeal.
4. Place fish strips in the air crisper basket and spray with olive oil.
5. Air crisp for 1012 minutes, until golden and crispy.
6. In a bowl, mix shredded cabbage, mayonnaise, lime juice, chopped cilantro, salt, and pepper.
7. Serve fish strips in tortillas with cabbage slaw.

Nutritional Info: Calories: 450 | Fat: 20g | Carbs: 40g | Protein: 25g

Cajun Shrimp Boil Foil Packs

Prep: 10 mins | Cook: 20 mins | Serves: 4

Ingredients:

- US: 1 lb large shrimp (peeled and deveined), 2 ears corn (cut into chunks), 1/2 lb baby potatoes (halved), 1 smoked sausage (sliced), 2 tablespoons Cajun seasoning, 2 tablespoons butter (melted), salt, pepper, lemon wedges
- UK: 500g large shrimp (peeled and deveined), 2 ears corn (cut into chunks), 250g baby potatoes (halved), 1 smoked sausage (sliced), 2 tablespoons Cajun seasoning, 30g butter (melted), salt, pepper, lemon wedges

Instructions:

1. Preheat the Ninja Foodi using the BAKE/ROAST function at 400°F (200°C).
2. In a large bowl, mix shrimp, corn, potatoes, sausage, Cajun seasoning, melted butter, salt, and pepper.
3. Divide the mixture among four pieces of foil and seal packets.
4. Place foil packs in the Ninja Foodi pot.
5. Bake/roast for 1520 minutes, until potatoes are tender and shrimp are cooked through.
6. Serve with lemon wedges.

Nutritional Info: Calories: 500 | Fat: 25g | Carbs: 35g | Protein: 30g

Tuna Poke Bowls with Avocado

Prep: 20 mins | Cook: 0 mins | Serves: 4

Ingredients:

- US: 1 lb sushi-grade tuna (cubed), 1 avocado (diced), 2 cups cooked rice, 1/4 cup soy sauce, 1 tablespoon sesame oil, 1 tablespoon rice vinegar, 1 teaspoon honey, 2 green onions (sliced), 1 tablespoon sesame seeds, salt, pepper
- UK: 500g sushi-grade tuna (cubed), 1 avocado (diced), 2 cups cooked rice, 60ml soy sauce, 1 tablespoon sesame oil, 1 tablespoon rice vinegar, 1 teaspoon honey, 2 spring onions (sliced), 1 tablespoon sesame seeds, salt, pepper

Instructions:

1. In a bowl, mix soy sauce, sesame oil, rice vinegar, honey, salt, and pepper.
2. Add cubed tuna to the bowl and let marinate for 10 minutes.
3. Divide cooked rice among four bowls.
4. Top with marinated tuna, diced avocado, sliced green onions, and sesame seeds.
5. Serve immediately.

Nutritional Info: Calories: 450 | Fat: 20g | Carbs: 35g | Protein: 30g

Baked Cod with Tomato and Olive Tapenade

Prep: 10 mins | Cook: 20 mins | Serves: 4

Ingredients:

- US: 4 cod fillets, 1/2 cup cherry tomatoes (halved), 1/4 cup black olives (chopped), 2 tablespoons capers, 2 tablespoons olive oil, 1 lemon (juiced), 2 cloves garlic (minced), salt, pepper, fresh basil (for garnish)
- UK: 4 cod fillets, 60g cherry tomatoes (halved), 60g black olives (chopped), 2 tablespoons capers, 30ml olive oil, 1 lemon (juiced), 2 cloves garlic (minced), salt, pepper, fresh basil (for garnish)

Instructions:

1. Preheat the Ninja Foodi using the BAKE/ROAST function at 375°F (190°C).
2. In a bowl, mix cherry tomatoes, black olives, capers, olive oil, lemon juice, minced garlic, salt, and pepper.
3. Place cod fillets on the rack inside the pot.
4. Top each fillet with the tomato and olive tapenade.
5. Bake/roast for 1520 minutes, until cod is flaky and cooked through.
6. Garnish with fresh basil and serve.

Nutritional Info: Calories: 300 | Fat: 15g | Carbs: 10g | Protein: 30g

Shrimp Fried Rice

Prep: 10 mins | Cook: 15 mins | Serves: 4

Ingredients:

- US: 1 lb shrimp (peeled and deveined), 2 cups cooked rice, 1 cup frozen peas and carrots, 2 eggs (beaten), 3 tablespoons soy sauce, 2 tablespoons vegetable oil, 2 cloves garlic (minced), 1 teaspoon ginger (grated), 2 green onions (sliced), salt, pepper
- UK: 500g shrimp (peeled and deveined), 2 cups cooked rice, 1 cup frozen peas and carrots, 2 eggs (beaten), 3 tablespoons soy sauce, 2 tablespoons vegetable oil, 2 cloves garlic (minced), 1 teaspoon ginger (grated), 2 spring onions (sliced), salt, pepper

Instructions:

1. Preheat the Ninja Foodi using the SAUTÉ function.
2. Add vegetable oil to the pot. Once hot, add shrimp and cook until pink. Remove and set aside.
3. Add minced garlic and grated ginger, sauté until fragrant.
4. Add cooked rice, frozen peas, and carrots. Stir to combine.
5. Create a well in the center and pour in beaten eggs. Scramble until cooked.
6. Return shrimp to the pot and stir in soy sauce, salt, and pepper.
7. Garnish with sliced green onions and serve hot.

Nutritional Info: Calories: 450 | Fat: 15g | Carbs: 50g | Protein: 25g

Blackened Mahi Mahi with Mango Salsa

Prep: 10 mins | Cook: 10 mins | Serves: 4

Ingredients:

- US: 4 mahi mahi fillets, 2 tablespoons blackening seasoning, 2 tablespoons olive oil, 1 mango (diced), 1/4 red onion (diced), 1/2 jalapeño (seeded and minced), 1/4 cup cilantro (chopped), 1 lime (juiced), salt, pepper
- UK: 4 mahi mahi fillets, 2 tablespoons blackening seasoning, 30ml olive oil, 1 mango (diced), 1/4 red onion (diced), 1/2 jalapeño (seeded and minced), 60ml cilantro (chopped), 1 lime (juiced), salt, pepper

Instructions:

1. Preheat the Ninja Foodi using the AIR CRISP function at 400°F (200°C).
2. Rub mahi mahi fillets with blackening seasoning.
3. Place fillets in the air crisper basket and spray with olive oil.
4. Air crisp for 810 minutes, until fish is cooked through.
5. In a bowl, mix diced mango, red onion, jalapeño, chopped cilantro, lime juice, salt, and pepper.
6. Serve blackened mahi mahi topped with mango salsa.

Nutritional Info: Calories: 350 | Fat: 18g | Carbs: 20g | Protein: 25g

Prep: 20 mins | Cook: 1 hour | Serves: 6

Ingredients:

- US: 1/2 lb shrimp (peeled and deveined), 1/2 lb crab meat, 1/2 lb andouille sausage (sliced), 1/2 cup flour, 1/2 cup vegetable oil, 1 onion (chopped), 1 bell pepper (chopped), 2 celery stalks (chopped), 4 cloves garlic (minced), 4 cups chicken broth, 1 can diced tomatoes, 1 tablespoon Cajun seasoning, 1 bay leaf, 2 cups okra (sliced), 2 green onions (sliced), salt, pepper, cooked rice (for serving)
- UK: 250g shrimp (peeled and deveined), 250g crab meat, 250g andouille sausage (sliced), 60g flour, 60ml vegetable oil, 1 onion (chopped), 1 bell pepper (chopped), 2 celery stalks (chopped), 4 cloves garlic (minced), 1 liter chicken broth, 1 can diced tomatoes, 1 tablespoon Cajun seasoning, 1 bay leaf, 200g okra (sliced), 2 spring onions (sliced), salt, pepper, cooked rice (for serving)

Instructions:

1. Preheat the Ninja Foodi using the SAUTÉ function.
2. Make a roux by whisking flour and vegetable oil together until it turns a dark brown color.
3. Add chopped onion, bell pepper, celery, and minced garlic. Sauté until vegetables are tender.
4. Stir in chicken broth, diced tomatoes, Cajun seasoning, and bay leaf.
5. Add sliced sausage, okra, and bring to a simmer.
6. Close the lid and set to PRESSURE COOK on high for 30 minutes.
7. Once the cooking cycle is complete, perform a quick release of the pressure.
8. Add shrimp and crab meat, and let them cook in the hot gumbo until done.
9. Serve gumbo over cooked rice, garnished with sliced green onions.

Nutritional Info: Calories: 600 | Fat: 30g | Carbs: 50g | Protein: 30g

Prep: 15 mins | Cook: 10 mins | Serves: 4

Ingredients:

- US: 1 lb lump crab meat, 1/4 cup breadcrumbs, 1/4 cup mayonnaise, 1 egg, 2 green onions (sliced), 1 tablespoon Dijon mustard, 1 tablespoon Worcestershire sauce, 1 teaspoon Old Bay seasoning, 1/4 cup vegetable oil, 1/2 cup mayonnaise, 1 tablespoon capers (chopped), 1 tablespoon pickles (chopped), 1 tablespoon lemon juice, 1 teaspoon hot sauce, salt, pepper
- UK: 500g lump crab meat, 60g breadcrumbs, 60ml mayonnaise, 1 egg, 2 spring onions (sliced), 1 tablespoon Dijon mustard, 1 tablespoon Worcestershire sauce, 1 teaspoon Old Bay seasoning, 60ml vegetable oil, 120ml mayonnaise, 1 tablespoon capers (chopped), 1 tablespoon pickles (chopped), 1 tablespoon lemon juice, 1 teaspoon hot sauce, salt, pepper

Instructions:

1. In a bowl, mix crab meat, breadcrumbs, mayonnaise, egg, sliced green onions, Dijon mustard, Worcestershire sauce, Old Bay seasoning, salt, and pepper.

2. Form the mixture into patties.
3. Preheat the Ninja Foodi using the AIR CRISP function at 400°F (200°C).
4. Place crab cakes in the air crisper basket and spray with vegetable oil.
5. Air crisp for 810 minutes, until golden brown and crispy.
6. In a small bowl, mix mayonnaise, chopped capers, chopped pickles, lemon juice, hot sauce, salt, and pepper to make the remoulade sauce.
7. Serve crab cakes with remoulade sauce.

Nutritional Info: Calories: 400 | Fat: 25g | Carbs: 15g | Protein: 25g

CHAPTER 7: SIDE DISHES GALORE

Roasted Garlic Mashed Potatoes

Prep: 15 mins | Cook: 25 mins | Serves: 6

Ingredients:

- US: 2 lbs potatoes (peeled and cubed), 1 bulb garlic, 1/2 cup milk, 4 tablespoons butter, salt, pepper, 1 tablespoon olive oil
- UK: 1 kg potatoes (peeled and cubed), 1 bulb garlic, 120ml milk, 60g butter, salt, pepper, 1 tablespoon olive oil

Instructions:

1. Preheat the Ninja Foodi using the BAKE/ROAST function at 400°F (200°C).
2. Cut the top off the garlic bulb, drizzle with olive oil, and wrap in foil.
3. Roast garlic in the Ninja Foodi for 25 minutes until soft.
4. Meanwhile, place cubed potatoes in the Ninja Foodi pot, add water to cover, and salt.
5. Pressure cook on high for 10 minutes, then quick release.
6. Drain potatoes, add roasted garlic, milk, butter, salt, and pepper.
7. Mash until smooth and creamy. Serve hot.

Nutritional Info: Calories: 250 | Fat: 10g | Carbs: 35g | Protein: 4g

Honey Glazed Carrots and Parsnips

Prep: 10 mins | Cook: 25 mins | Serves: 4

Ingredients:

- US: 500g carrots (peeled and sliced into sticks), 500g parsnips (peeled and sliced into sticks), 2 tablespoons honey, 2 tablespoons olive oil, salt, pepper, chopped fresh parsley (for garnish)
- UK: 500g carrots (peeled and sliced into sticks), 500g parsnips (peeled and sliced into sticks), 2 tablespoons honey, 2 tablespoons olive oil, salt, pepper, chopped fresh parsley (for garnish)

Instructions:

1. Preheat the Ninja Foodi using the AIR CRISP function at 375°F (190°C).
2. In a large bowl, toss carrots and parsnips with olive oil, honey, salt, and pepper.
3. Place the vegetables in the air crisper basket.
4. Air crisp for 2025 minutes, shaking the basket halfway through, until tender and caramelized.
5. Garnish with chopped fresh parsley and serve.

Nutritional Info: Calories: 180 | Fat: 7g | Carbs: 29g | Protein: 2g

Loaded Baked Potato Wedges

Prep: 15 mins | Cook: 25 mins | Serves: 4

Ingredients:

- US: 4 large potatoes, 2 tablespoons olive oil, 1 teaspoon garlic powder, 1 teaspoon onion powder, 1/2 cup shredded cheddar cheese, 4 slices bacon (cooked and crumbled), 2 green onions (sliced), salt, pepper, sour cream (for serving)
- UK: 4 large potatoes, 2 tablespoons olive oil, 1 teaspoon garlic powder, 1 teaspoon onion powder, 60g shredded cheddar cheese, 4 slices bacon (cooked and crumbled), 2 spring onions (sliced), salt, pepper, sour cream (for serving)

Instructions:

1. Preheat the Ninja Foodi using the AIR CRISP function at 400°F (200°C).
2. Cut potatoes into wedges and toss with olive oil, garlic powder, onion powder, salt, and pepper.
3. Place wedges in the air crisper basket.
4. Air crisp for 20 minutes, shaking the basket halfway through.
5. Sprinkle shredded cheddar and crumbled bacon over the wedges. Air crisp for another 5 minutes until cheese is melted.
6. Garnish with sliced green onions and serve with sour cream.

Nutritional Info: Calories: 350 | Fat: 18g | Carbs: 40g | Protein: 10g

Sautéed Green Beans with Almonds

Prep: 10 mins | Cook: 15 mins | Serves: 4

Ingredients:

- US: 1 lb green beans (trimmed), 2 tablespoons butter, 1/4 cup sliced almonds, 2 cloves garlic (minced), salt, pepper, 1 lemon (zested and juiced)
- UK: 500g green beans (trimmed), 30g butter, 60g sliced almonds, 2 cloves garlic (minced), salt, pepper, 1 lemon (zested and juiced)

Instructions:

1. Preheat the Ninja Foodi using the SAUTÉ function.
2. Add butter to the pot and let it melt.
3. Add minced garlic and sauté until fragrant.
4. Add green beans and sauté for 10 minutes until tender.
5. Add sliced almonds, lemon zest, lemon juice, salt, and pepper.
6. Sauté for another 23 minutes until almonds are toasted.
7. Serve hot.

Nutritional Info: Calories: 150 | Fat: 11g | Carbs: 10g | Protein: 4g

Macaroni and Cheese with Breadcrumb Topping

Prep: 10 mins | Cook: 20 mins | Serves: 6

Ingredients:
- US: 2 cups macaroni, 2 cups milk, 2 cups shredded cheddar cheese, 2 tablespoons butter, 1/4 cup breadcrumbs, 1 tablespoon flour, salt, pepper
- UK: 200g macaroni, 500ml milk, 200g shredded cheddar cheese, 30g butter, 60g breadcrumbs, 1 tablespoon flour, salt, pepper

Instructions:
1. Preheat the Ninja Foodi using the SAUTÉ function.
2. Add butter to the pot and let it melt. Stir in flour to make a roux.
3. Slowly add milk while whisking continuously until the mixture thickens.
4. Add shredded cheddar cheese, salt, and pepper, stirring until the cheese is melted and the sauce is smooth.
5. Stir in cooked macaroni until well combined.
6. Sprinkle breadcrumbs over the top.
7. Switch to the BAKE/ROAST function at 375°F (190°C) and cook for 10 minutes until the top is golden and bubbly.
8. Serve hot.

Nutritional Info: Calories: 400 | Fat: 20g | Carbs: 40g | Protein: 15g

Roasted Brussels Sprouts with Bacon

Prep: 10 mins | Cook: 20 mins | Serves: 4

Ingredients:
- US: 1 lb Brussels sprouts (halved), 4 slices bacon (chopped), 2 tablespoons olive oil, salt, pepper, 1 tablespoon balsamic vinegar
- UK: 500g Brussels sprouts (halved), 4 slices bacon (chopped), 30ml olive oil, salt, pepper, 1 tablespoon balsamic vinegar

Instructions:
1. Preheat the Ninja Foodi using the AIR CRISP function at 400°F (200°C).
2. In a large bowl, toss Brussels sprouts with olive oil, salt, and pepper.
3. Place Brussels sprouts and chopped bacon in the air crisper basket.
4. Air crisp for 1520 minutes, shaking the basket halfway through, until sprouts are crispy and bacon is cooked.
5. Drizzle with balsamic vinegar before serving.

Nutritional Info: Calories: 250 | Fat: 18g | Carbs: 15g | Protein: 10g

Cilantro Lime Rice

Prep: 5 mins | Cook: 20 mins | Serves: 4

Ingredients:

- US: 1 cup long-grain white rice, 2 cups water, 1/4 cup fresh cilantro (chopped), 1 lime (zested and juiced), 1 tablespoon olive oil, salt
- UK: 200g long-grain white rice, 500ml water, 60ml fresh cilantro (chopped), 1 lime (zested and juiced), 1 tablespoon olive oil, salt

Instructions:

1. Place rice, water, and salt in the Ninja Foodi pot.
2. Pressure cook on high for 5 minutes, then natural release for 10 minutes.
3. Fluff rice with a fork and stir in chopped cilantro, lime zest, lime juice, and olive oil.
4. Serve hot.

Nutritional Info: Calories: 200 | Fat: 5g | Carbs: 35g | Protein: 4g

Baked Sweet Potato Fries

Prep: 10 mins | Cook: 25 mins | Serves: 4

Ingredients:

- US: 3 large sweet potatoes (peeled and cut into fries), 2 tablespoons olive oil, 1 teaspoon paprika, 1 teaspoon garlic powder, salt, pepper
- UK: 3 large sweet potatoes (peeled and cut into fries), 30ml olive oil, 1 teaspoon paprika, 1 teaspoon garlic powder, salt, pepper

Instructions:

1. Preheat the Ninja Foodi using the AIR CRISP function at 400°F (200°C).
2. In a large bowl, toss sweet potato fries with olive oil, paprika, garlic powder, salt, and pepper.
3. Place fries in the air crisper basket.
4. Air crisp for 2025 minutes, shaking the basket halfway through, until fries are crispy.
5. Serve hot.

Nutritional Info: Calories: 180 | Fat: 7g | Carbs: 30g | Protein: 2g

Garlic Parmesan Roasted Asparagus

Prep: 5 mins | Cook: 10 mins | Serves: 4

Ingredients:

- US: 1 lb asparagus (trimmed), 2 tablespoons olive oil, 1/4 cup grated Parmesan cheese, 2 cloves garlic (minced), salt, pepper
- UK: 500g asparagus (trimmed), 30ml olive oil, 60g grated Parmesan cheese, 2 cloves garlic (minced), salt, pepper

Instructions:

1. Preheat the Ninja Foodi using the AIR CRISP function at 400°F (200°C).
2. In a large bowl, toss asparagus with olive oil, minced garlic, salt, and pepper.
3. Place asparagus in the air crisper basket.
4. Air crisp for 810 minutes until tender and slightly crispy.
5. Sprinkle with grated Parmesan cheese before serving.

Nutritional Info: Calories: 120 | Fat: 8g | Carbs: 5g | Protein: 6g

Cheesy Cauliflower Bake

Prep: 10 mins | Cook: 25 mins | Serves: 6

Ingredients:

- US: 1 large head cauliflower (cut into florets), 1 cup shredded cheddar cheese, 1/2 cup heavy cream, 2 tablespoons butter, 1/4 cup breadcrumbs, salt, pepper
- UK: 1 large head cauliflower (cut into florets), 100g shredded cheddar cheese, 120ml heavy cream, 30g butter, 60g breadcrumbs, salt, pepper

Instructions:

1. Preheat the Ninja Foodi using the BAKE/ROAST function at 375°F (190°C).
2. Steam cauliflower florets using the STEAM function for 5 minutes.
3. Drain cauliflower and place in a baking dish.
4. In a saucepan, melt butter and stir in heavy cream and shredded cheddar cheese until smooth.
5. Pour cheese sauce over cauliflower and sprinkle with breadcrumbs.
6. Bake for 20 minutes until golden and bubbly.
7. Serve hot.

Nutritional Info: Calories: 250 | Fat: 20g | Carbs: 10g | Protein: 8g

CHAPTER 8: BREADS AND BAKED GOODS

Homemade Dinner Rolls

Prep: 15 mins | Cook: 25 mins | Serves: 12 rolls

Ingredients:
- US: 240ml warm milk, 50g sugar, 2 1/4 tsp active dry yeast, 2 large eggs, 60g butter (melted), 1 tsp salt, 500g all-purpose flour, Butter (for brushing)
- UK: 240ml warm milk, 50g sugar, 2 1/4 tsp active dry yeast, 2 large eggs, 60g butter (melted), 1 tsp salt, 500g plain flour, Butter (for brushing)

Instructions:
1. In a large bowl, combine warm milk and sugar. Sprinkle the yeast on top and let it sit for 510 minutes until frothy.
2. Add eggs, melted butter, and salt to the yeast mixture. Mix well.
3. Gradually add flour, mixing until a soft dough forms.
4. Knead the dough on a floured surface for about 10 minutes, until smooth and elastic.
5. Place the dough in a greased bowl, cover, and let rise for 1 hour or until doubled in size.
6. Divide the dough into 12 equal pieces and shape into rolls.
7. Place the rolls in the greased baking dish of your Ninja Foodi.
8. Select the BAKE/ROAST function, set to 180°C (350°F), and bake for 25 minutes or until golden brown.
9. Brush the tops with melted butter and serve warm.

Nutritional Info: Calories: 170 | Fat: 5g | Carbs: 28g | Protein: 5g

Banana Bread with Walnuts

Prep: 10 mins | Cook: 1 hour | Serves: 1 loaf

Ingredients:
- US: 3 ripe bananas (mashed), 150g sugar, 1 large egg, 60ml vegetable oil, 1 tsp vanilla extract, 190g all-purpose flour, 1 tsp baking soda, 1/2 tsp salt, 100g chopped walnuts
- UK: 3 ripe bananas (mashed), 150g sugar, 1 large egg, 60ml vegetable oil, 1 tsp vanilla extract, 190g plain flour, 1 tsp bicarbonate of soda, 1/2 tsp salt, 100g chopped walnuts

Instructions:
1. In a large bowl, mix mashed bananas, sugar, egg, vegetable oil, and vanilla extract until well combined.
2. In another bowl, whisk together flour, baking soda, and salt.
3. Gradually add dry ingredients to the banana mixture, stirring until just combined.
4. Fold in the chopped walnuts.
5. Pour the batter into a greased loaf pan.

6. Place the pan in your Ninja Foodi, select BAKE/ROAST, set to 160°C (320°F), and bake for 1 hour or until a toothpick inserted in the center comes out clean.
7. Let the bread cool in the pan for 10 minutes before transferring to a wire rack to cool completely.

Nutritional Info: Calories: 220 | Fat: 10g | Carbs: 31g | Protein: 4g

Cheddar and Chive Biscuits

Prep: 15 mins | Cook: 15 mins | Serves: 8 biscuits

Ingredients:
- US: 240g all-purpose flour, 1 tbsp baking powder, 1/2 tsp salt, 60g cold butter (cubed), 120g shredded cheddar cheese, 2 tbsp chopped fresh chives, 180ml milk
- UK: 240g plain flour, 1 tbsp baking powder, 1/2 tsp salt, 60g cold butter (cubed), 120g shredded cheddar cheese, 2 tbsp chopped fresh chives, 180ml milk

Instructions:
1. Preheat your Ninja Foodi using the BAKE/ROAST function, set to 220°C (425°F).
2. In a large bowl, combine flour, baking powder, and salt.
3. Cut in the cold butter until the mixture resembles coarse crumbs.
4. Stir in the cheddar cheese and chives.
5. Gradually add milk, stirring just until the dough comes together.
6. Turn the dough out onto a floured surface and knead gently a few times.
7. Roll out the dough to about 1inch thickness and cut into 8 biscuits using a biscuit cutter.
8. Place the biscuits on the greased baking tray of your Ninja Foodi.
9. Bake for 1215 minutes or until golden brown.

Nutritional Info: Calories: 190 | Fat: 10g | Carbs: 21g | Protein: 5g

Focaccia Bread with Rosemary and Garlic

Prep: 20 mins | Cook: 25 mins | Serves: 1 loaf

Ingredients:
- US: 500g all-purpose flour, 10g salt, 7g instant yeast, 300ml warm water, 60ml olive oil (divided), 3 garlic cloves (minced), 2 tbsp fresh rosemary leaves, Coarse sea salt
- UK: 500g plain flour, 10g salt, 7g instant yeast, 300ml warm water, 60ml olive oil (divided), 3 garlic cloves (minced), 2 tbsp fresh rosemary leaves, Coarse sea salt

Instructions:
1. In a large bowl, mix flour, salt, and yeast.
2. Gradually add warm water and 30ml olive oil, mixing until a sticky dough forms.
3. Knead the dough on a floured surface for about 10 minutes until smooth and elastic.
4. Place the dough in a greased bowl, cover, and let rise for 1 hour or until doubled in size.
5. Preheat your Ninja Foodi using the BAKE/ROAST function, set to 200°C (400°F).
6. Stretch the dough into a greased baking pan.

7. Drizzle the remaining olive oil over the dough, then sprinkle with minced garlic, rosemary leaves, and coarse sea salt.
8. Use your fingers to dimple the surface of the dough.
9. Bake for 25 minutes or until golden brown.

Nutritional Info: Calories: 250 | Fat: 10g | Carbs: 36g | Protein: 5g

Zucchini Bread with Lemon Glaze

Prep: 15 mins | Cook: 50 mins | Serves: 1 loaf

Ingredients:

- US: 250g grated zucchini, 150g sugar, 2 large eggs, 125ml vegetable oil, 1 tsp vanilla extract, 250g all-purpose flour, 1 tsp baking soda, 1/2 tsp baking powder, 1/2 tsp salt, Zest of 1 lemon, 120g powdered sugar, Juice of 1 lemon
- UK: 250g grated zucchini, 150g sugar, 2 large eggs, 125ml vegetable oil, 1 tsp vanilla extract, 250g plain flour, 1 tsp bicarbonate of soda, 1/2 tsp baking powder, 1/2 tsp salt, Zest of 1 lemon, 120g icing sugar, Juice of 1 lemon

Instructions:

1. Preheat your Ninja Foodi using the BAKE/ROAST function, set to 175°C (350°F).
2. In a large bowl, mix grated zucchini, sugar, eggs, vegetable oil, and vanilla extract.
3. In another bowl, whisk together flour, baking soda, baking powder, salt, and lemon zest.
4. Gradually add dry ingredients to the zucchini mixture, stirring until just combined.
5. Pour the batter into a greased loaf pan.
6. Place the pan in your Ninja Foodi and bake for 50 minutes or until a toothpick inserted in the center comes out clean.
7. Let the bread cool in the pan for 10 minutes before transferring to a wire rack.
8. For the glaze, mix powdered sugar and lemon juice until smooth. Drizzle over the cooled bread.

Nutritional Info: Calories: 280 | Fat: 12g | Carbs: 40g | Protein: 4g

Whole Wheat Pita Bread

Prep: 10 mins | Cook: 10 mins | Serves: 8 pitas

Ingredients:

- US: 240ml warm water, 1 tsp sugar, 2 1/4 tsp active dry yeast, 240g whole wheat flour, 120g all-purpose flour, 1 tsp salt, 30ml olive oil
- UK: 240ml warm water, 1 tsp sugar, 2 1/4 tsp active dry yeast, 240g whole wheat flour, 120g plain flour, 1 tsp salt, 30ml olive oil

Instructions:

1. In a large bowl, combine warm water and sugar. Sprinkle the yeast on top and let it sit for 510 minutes until frothy.
2. Add whole wheat flour, all-purpose flour, salt, and olive oil to the yeast mixture. Mix until a dough forms.
3. Knead the dough on a floured surface for about 5 minutes until smooth and elastic.
4. Place the dough in a greased bowl, cover, and let rise for 1 hour or until doubled in size.
5. Preheat your Ninja Foodi using the AIR FRY function, set to 200°C (390°F).
6. Divide the dough into 8 equal pieces and roll each into a ball. Flatten each ball into a round pita.
7. Place the pitas in the greased baking tray of your Ninja Foodi.
8. Bake for 10 minutes or until puffed and golden brown.

Nutritional Info: Calories: 150 | Fat: 4g | Carbs: 26g | Protein: 4g

Strawberry Cream Scones

Prep: 15 mins | Cook: 20 mins | Serves: 8 scones

Ingredients:

- US: 250g all-purpose flour, 50g sugar, 2 tsp baking powder, 1/4 tsp salt, 85g cold butter (cubed), 120g chopped strawberries, 180ml heavy cream, 1 tsp vanilla extract, 2 tbsp milk (for brushing), Sugar (for sprinkling)
- UK: 250g plain flour, 50g sugar, 2 tsp baking powder, 1/4 tsp salt, 85g cold butter (cubed), 120g chopped strawberries, 180ml double cream, 1 tsp vanilla extract, 2 tbsp milk (for brushing), Sugar (for sprinkling)

Instructions:

1. Preheat your Ninja Foodi using the BAKE/ROAST function, set to 200°C (400°F).
2. In a large bowl, combine flour, sugar, baking powder, and salt.
3. Cut in the cold butter until the mixture resembles coarse crumbs.
4. Gently fold in the chopped strawberries.
5. In a small bowl, mix heavy cream and vanilla extract.
6. Gradually add the cream mixture to the flour mixture, stirring until just combined.
7. Turn the dough out onto a floured surface and knead gently a few times.
8. Pat the dough into a 1inch thick circle and cut into 8 wedges.

9. Place the scones on the greased baking tray of your Ninja Foodi.
10. Brush the tops with milk and sprinkle with sugar.
11. Bake for 1520 minutes or until golden brown.

Nutritional Info: Calories: 220 | Fat: 12g | Carbs: 26g | Protein: 4g

Cornbread Muffins with Honey Butter

Prep: 10 mins | Cook: 15 mins | Serves: 12 muffins

Ingredients:
- US: 180g cornmeal, 125g all-purpose flour, 50g sugar, 1 tbsp baking powder, 1/2 tsp salt, 240ml milk, 60g melted butter, 2 large eggs, 60g honey, 120g softened butter
- UK: 180g cornmeal, 125g plain flour, 50g sugar, 1 tbsp baking powder, 1/2 tsp salt, 240ml milk, 60g melted butter, 2 large eggs, 60g honey, 120g softened butter

Instructions:
1. Preheat your Ninja Foodi using the BAKE/ROAST function, set to 200°C (400°F).
2. In a large bowl, combine cornmeal, flour, sugar, baking powder, and salt.
3. In another bowl, mix milk, melted butter, and eggs until well combined.
4. Gradually add the wet ingredients to the dry ingredients, stirring until just combined.
5. Pour the batter into greased muffin tins, filling each about 2/3 full.
6. Place the muffin tin in your Ninja Foodi and bake for 15 minutes or until a toothpick inserted in the center comes out clean.
7. For the honey butter, mix softened butter and honey until smooth.
8. Serve the warm cornbread muffins with honey butter.

Nutritional Info: Calories: 180 | Fat: 8g | Carbs: 25g | Protein: 3g

Garlic Knots

Prep: 15 mins | Cook: 15 mins | Serves: 12 knots

Ingredients:
- US: 250g all-purpose flour, 1 tsp sugar, 1 tsp salt, 2 1/4 tsp active dry yeast, 180ml warm water, 30ml olive oil, 60g melted butter, 3 garlic cloves (minced), 2 tbsp chopped fresh parsley
- UK: 250g plain flour, 1 tsp sugar, 1 tsp salt, 2 1/4 tsp active dry yeast, 180ml warm water, 30ml olive oil, 60g melted butter, 3 garlic cloves (minced), 2 tbsp chopped fresh parsley

Instructions:
1. In a large bowl, combine warm water and sugar. Sprinkle the yeast on top and let it sit for 510 minutes until frothy.
2. Add flour, salt, and olive oil to the yeast mixture. Mix until a dough forms.
3. Knead the dough on a floured surface for about 5 minutes until smooth and elastic.
4. Place the dough in a greased bowl, cover, and let rise for 1 hour or until doubled in size.
5. Preheat your Ninja Foodi using the BAKE/ROAST function, set to 200°C (400°F).
6. Divide the dough into 12 equal pieces and roll each into a rope. Tie each rope into a knot.

7. Place the knots on the greased baking tray of your Ninja Foodi.
8. Bake for 15 minutes or until golden brown.
9. In a small bowl, mix melted butter, minced garlic, and chopped parsley.
10. Brush the garlic butter over the warm knots before serving.

Nutritional Info: Calories: 130 | Fat: 6g | Carbs: 16g | Protein: 3g

Blueberry Lemon Bread

Prep: 15 mins | Cook: 1 hour | Serves: 1 loaf

Ingredients:

- US: 250g all-purpose flour, 150g sugar, 1 tsp baking powder, 1/2 tsp salt, 2 large eggs, 120ml milk, 60g melted butter, Zest of 1 lemon, 150g fresh blueberries, 120g powdered sugar, Juice of 1 lemon
- UK: 250g plain flour, 150g sugar, 1 tsp baking powder, 1/2 tsp salt, 2 large eggs, 120ml milk, 60g melted butter, Zest of 1 lemon, 150g fresh blueberries, 120g icing sugar, Juice of 1 lemon

Instructions:

1. Preheat your Ninja Foodi using the BAKE/ROAST function, set to 175°C (350°F).
2. In a large bowl, mix flour, sugar, baking powder, and salt.
3. In another bowl, whisk together eggs, milk, melted butter, and lemon zest.
4. Gradually add the wet ingredients to the dry ingredients, stirring until just combined.
5. Fold in the fresh blueberries.
6. Pour the batter into a greased loaf pan.
7. Place the pan in your Ninja Foodi and bake for 1 hour or until a toothpick inserted in the center comes out clean.
8. Let the bread cool in the pan for 10 minutes before transferring to a wire rack.
9. For the glaze, mix powdered sugar and lemon juice until smooth. Drizzle over the cooled bread.

Nutritional Info: Calories: 250 | Fat: 8g | Carbs: 42g | Protein: 4g

Chocolate Lava Cakes

Prep: 15 mins | Cook: 10 mins | Serves: 4

Ingredients:

- US: 170g semisweet chocolate (chopped), 113g unsalted butter, 100g powdered sugar, 2 large eggs, 2 large egg yolks, 30g all-purpose flour, Vanilla ice cream (for serving)
- UK: 170g semisweet chocolate (chopped), 113g unsalted butter, 100g icing sugar, 2 large eggs, 2 large egg yolks, 30g plain flour, Vanilla ice cream (for serving)

Instructions:

1. Melt the chocolate and butter together in a microwave-safe bowl in 30second intervals, stirring until smooth.
2. Stir in the powdered sugar until well combined.
3. Add the eggs and egg yolks, mixing well.
4. Stir in the flour until just combined.
5. Grease four ramekins and divide the batter evenly among them.
6. Place the ramekins on the rack inside your Ninja Foodi.
7. Select the PRESSURE COOK function, set to HIGH, and cook for 10 minutes.
8. Quick release the pressure and carefully remove the ramekins.
9. Invert the cakes onto plates and serve immediately with vanilla ice cream.

Nutritional Info: Calories: 350 | Fat: 22g | Carbs: 36g | Protein: 5g

New YorkStyle Cheesecake

Prep: 20 mins | Cook: 1 hour 10 mins | Serves: 8

Ingredients:

- US: 200g graham cracker crumbs, 75g melted butter, 900g cream cheese, 200g sugar, 240ml sour cream, 3 large eggs, 1 tsp vanilla extract
- UK: 200g digestive biscuit crumbs, 75g melted butter, 900g cream cheese, 200g sugar, 240ml sour cream, 3 large eggs, 1 tsp vanilla extract

Instructions:

1. Mix the graham cracker crumbs with melted butter and press into the bottom of a greased spring--form pan.
2. In a large bowl, beat the cream cheese and sugar until smooth.
3. Add sour cream, eggs, and vanilla extract, bea-ting until well combined.
4. Pour the mixture over the crust in the spring-form pan.
5. Cover the pan with foil and place on the rack inside your Ninja Foodi.
6. Select the STEAM & CRISP function, set to 325°F (165°C), and cook for 1 hour 10 minutes.
7. Let the cheesecake cool, then refrigerate for at least 4 hours before serving.

Nutritional Info: Calories: 450 | Fat: 33g | Carbs: 30g | Protein: 7g

Apple Crisp with Oat Topping

Prep: 15 mins | Cook: 40 mins | Serves: 6

Ingredients:

- US: 5 large apples (peeled, cored, and sliced), 100g sugar, 1 tsp cinnamon, 150g rolled oats, 100g brown sugar, 75g flour, 113g butter (cubed)
- UK: 5 large apples (peeled, cored, and sliced), 100g sugar, 1 tsp cinnamon, 150g rolled oats, 100g brown sugar, 75g flour, 113g butter (cubed)

Instructions:

1. Preheat your Ninja Foodi using the BAKE/ROAST function, set to 175°C (350°F).
2. In a large bowl, mix apples with sugar and cinnamon. Place in a greased baking dish.
3. In another bowl, combine oats, brown sugar, and flour. Cut in the butter until the mixture resembles coarse crumbs.
4. Sprinkle the oat mixture over the apples.
5. Place the baking dish in your Ninja Foodi and bake for 40 minutes or until the topping is golden and the apples are tender.
6. Serve warm, optionally with a scoop of vanilla ice cream.

Nutritional Info: Calories: 320 | Fat: 12g | Carbs: 54g | Protein: 3g

Molten Chocolate Pudding Cakes

Prep: 15 mins | Cook: 12 mins | Serves: 4

Ingredients:

- US: 120g dark chocolate, 113g unsalted butter, 100g powdered sugar, 2 large eggs, 2 large egg yolks, 30g all-purpose -flour
- UK: 120g dark chocolate, 113g unsalted butter, 100g icing sugar, 2 large eggs, 2 large egg yolks, 30g plain flour

Instructions:

1. Melt the chocolate and butter together in a microwave-safe bowl in 30second intervals, stirring until smooth.
2. Stir in the powdered sugar until well combined.
3. Add the eggs and egg yolks, mixing well.
4. Stir in the flour until just combined.
5. Grease four ramekins and divide the batter evenly among them.
6. Place the ramekins on the rack inside your Ninja Foodi.
7. Select the PRESSURE COOK function, set to HIGH, and cook for 12 minutes.
8. Quick release the pressure and carefully remove the ramekins.
9. Serve warm, optionally with a dollop of whipped cream.

Nutritional Info: Calories: 360 | Fat: 24g | Carbs: 35g | Protein: 5g

Lemon Bars with Shortbread Crust

Prep: 20 mins | Cook: 40 mins | Serves: 12 bars

Ingredients:

- US: 150g all-purpose flour, 50g powdered sugar, 113g cold butter (cubed), 200g sugar, 3 large eggs, 120ml lemon juice, Zest of 1 lemon
- UK: 150g plain flour, 50g icing sugar, 113g cold butter (cubed), 200g sugar, 3 large eggs, 120ml lemon juice, Zest of 1 lemon

Instructions:

1. Preheat your Ninja Foodi using the BAKE/ROAST function, set to 175°C (350°F).
2. In a bowl, mix flour and powdered sugar. Cut in the cold butter until the mixture resembles coarse crumbs.
3. Press the mixture into the bottom of a greased baking dish.
4. Bake the crust for 15 minutes or until lightly golden.
5. In another bowl, whisk together sugar, eggs, lemon juice, and lemon zest.
6. Pour the lemon mixture over the baked crust.
7. Place the baking dish back in your Ninja Foodi and bake for 25 minutes or until the filling is set.
8. Let the bars cool completely before cutting into squares.

Nutritional Info: Calories: 220 | Fat: 10g | Carbs: 30g | Protein: 3g

Peanut Butter Cups

Prep: 10 mins | Cook: 20 mins | Serves: 12 cups

Ingredients:

- US: 300g semisweet chocolate (chopped), 150g creamy peanut butter, 50g powdered sugar, 1 tsp vanilla extract
- UK: 300g semisweet chocolate (chopped), 150g creamy peanut butter, 50g icing sugar, 1 tsp vanilla extract

Instructions:

1. Melt the chocolate in a microwavesafe bowl in 30second intervals, stirring until smooth.
2. In another bowl, mix peanut butter, powdered sugar, and vanilla extract until smooth.
3. Line a muffin tin with paper liners.
4. Spoon a small amount of melted chocolate into each liner and spread it to cover the bottom.
5. Add a spoonful of the peanut butter mixture on top of the chocolate layer.
6. Cover the peanut butter layer with more melted chocolate.
7. Place the muffin tin in the refrigerator for 20 minutes or until the chocolate is set.
8. Remove the paper liners and enjoy your homemade peanut butter cups.

Nutritional Info: Calories: 200 | Fat: 14g | Carbs: 18g | Protein: 4g

Pecan Pie Bites

Prep: 20 mins | Cook: 25 mins | Serves: 24 bites

Ingredients:
- US: 150g all-purpose flour, 75g powdered sugar, 113g cold butter (cubed), 200g chopped pecans, 100g brown sugar, 120ml corn syrup, 2 large eggs, 1 tsp vanilla extract
- UK: 150g plain flour, 75g icing sugar, 113g cold butter (cubed), 200g chopped pecans, 100g brown sugar, 120ml golden syrup, 2 large eggs, 1 tsp vanilla extract

Instructions:
1. Preheat your Ninja Foodi using the BAKE/ROAST function, set to 175°C (350°F).
2. In a bowl, mix flour and powdered sugar. Cut in the cold butter until the mixture resembles coarse crumbs.
3. Press the mixture into the bottom of a greased mini muffin tin.
4. Bake the crust for 10 minutes or until lightly golden.
5. In another bowl, mix chopped pecans, brown sugar, corn syrup, eggs, and vanilla extract.
6. Spoon the pecan mixture into the prebaked crusts.
7. Place the muffin tin back in your Ninja Foodi and bake for 15 minutes or until the filling is set.
8. Let the bites cool before removing them from the tin.

Nutritional Info: Calories: 150 | Fat: 10g | Carbs: 15g | Protein: 2g

Strawberry Shortcake Trifles

Prep: 20 mins | Cook: 15 mins | Serves: 6

Ingredients:
- US: 200g all-purpose flour, 50g sugar, 1 tsp baking powder, 1/2 tsp salt, 113g cold butter (cubed), 120ml heavy cream, 500g strawberries (sliced), 100g sugar, 240ml whipped cream
- UK: 200g plain flour, 50g sugar, 1 tsp baking powder, 1/2 tsp salt, 113g cold butter (cubed), 120ml double cream, 500g strawberries (sliced), 100g sugar, 240ml whipped cream

Instructions:
1. Preheat your Ninja Foodi using the BAKE/ROAST function, set to 200°C (400°F).
2. In a bowl, mix flour, sugar, baking powder, and salt. Cut in the cold butter until the mixture resembles coarse crumbs.
3. Stir in the heavy cream until just combined.
4. Drop spoonfuls of the dough onto a greased baking tray.
5. Bake for 1215 minutes or until golden brown. Let cool.
6. In a bowl, mix sliced strawberries with sugar. Let sit for 10 minutes.
7. To assemble the trifles, layer pieces of shortcake, strawberries, and whipped cream in serving glasses.
8. Repeat the layers and serve immediately.

Nutritional Info: Calories: 350 | Fat: 18g | Carbs: 40g | Protein: 4g

Prep: 15 mins | Cook: 20 mins | Serves: 6

Ingredients:

- US: 250ml water, 120g butter, 1/4 tsp salt, 150g all-purpose flour, 3 large eggs, 100g sugar, 1 tsp cinnamon, 200g semisweet chocolate, 120ml heavy cream
- UK: 250ml water, 120g butter, 1/4 tsp salt, 150g plain flour, 3 large eggs, 100g sugar, 1 tsp cinnamon, 200g semisweet chocolate, 120ml double cream

Instructions:

1. In a saucepan, bring water, butter, and salt to a boil.
2. Remove from heat and stir in flour until the mixture forms a ball.
3. Let the mixture cool slightly, then beat in eggs one at a time.
4. Transfer the dough to a piping bag fitted with a star tip.
5. Preheat your Ninja Foodi using the AIR FRY function, set to 200°C (390°F).
6. Pipe churro dough into 4inch strips onto a parchment-lined tray.
7. Air fry the churros for 10 minutes or until golden and crispy.
8. In a small bowl, mix sugar and cinnamon. Roll the churros in the mixture while still warm.
9. For the chocolate sauce, melt the chocolate and cream together in a microwave-safe bowl, stirring until smooth.
10. Serve the churros with the chocolate sauce.

Nutritional Info: Calories: 300 | Fat: 20g | Carbs: 35g | Protein: 5g

Crème Brûlée

Prep: 15 mins | Cook: 35 mins | Serves: 4

Ingredients:

- US: 480ml heavy cream, 1 vanilla bean (split and scraped), 5 large egg yolks, 100g sugar, 50g sugar (for caramelizing)
- UK: 480ml double cream, 1 vanilla bean (split and scraped), 5 large egg yolks, 100g sugar, 50g sugar (for caramelizing)

Instructions:

1. In a saucepan, heat the cream and vanilla bean over medium heat until just boiling. Remove from heat and let sit for 15 minutes.
2. In a bowl, whisk egg yolks and sugar until pale and thick.
3. Gradually add the cream mixture to the egg yolk mixture, stirring constantly.
4. Strain the mixture through a fine sieve into a jug.
5. Pour the custard into four ramekins and place on the rack inside your Ninja Foodi.
6. Select the PRESSURE COOK function, set to LOW, and cook for 30 minutes.
7. Quick release the pressure and carefully remove the ramekins.
8. Chill the custards in the refrigerator for at least 2 hours.

9. Before serving, sprinkle sugar evenly over each custard and caramelize with a kitchen torch until golden and crisp.

Nutritional Info: Calories: 450 | Fat: 36g | Carbs: 30g | Protein: 5g

Homemade Marinara Sauce

Prep: 10 mins | Cook: 30 mins | Makes: 2 cups

Ingredients:

- US: 800g canned tomatoes, 30ml olive oil, 1 onion (chopped), 3 cloves garlic (minced), 1 teaspoon dried oregano, 1 teaspoon dried basil, salt, pepper
- UK: 800g canned tomatoes, 30ml olive oil, 1 onion (chopped), 3 cloves garlic (minced), 1 teaspoon dried oregano, 1 teaspoon dried basil, salt, pepper

Instructions:

1. Select Sauté function on the Ninja Foodi and heat olive oil.
2. Add chopped onion and minced garlic, cook until softened.
3. Stir in canned tomatoes, oregano, basil, salt, and pepper.
4. Close the lid, select Pressure Cook on High for 10 minutes.
5. Once done, allow pressure to release naturally for 5 minutes, then manually release.
6. Use a hand blender to blend until smooth.

Nutritional Info: Calories: 60 | Fat: 4g | Carbs: 6g | Protein: 1g

Creamy Avocado Dip

Prep: 10 mins | Cook: 0 mins | Makes: 1 cup

Ingredients:

- US: 2 ripe avocados, 1/4 cup Greek yogurt, 1 tablespoon lime juice, 1 clove garlic (minced), salt, pepper
- UK: 2 ripe avocados, 60g Greek yogurt, 1 tablespoon lime juice, 1 clove garlic (minced), salt, pepper

Instructions:

1. Scoop out avocado flesh into a bowl.
2. Add Greek yogurt, lime juice, minced garlic, salt, and pepper.
3. Mash and mix until creamy.
4. Serve immediately or refrigerate until ready to use.

Nutritional Info: Calories: 120 | Fat: 10g | Carbs: 7g | Protein: 3g

Tzatziki Sauce

Prep: 15 mins | Cook: 0 mins | Makes: 1 cup

Ingredients:

- US: 1 cucumber (seeded and grated), 240ml Greek yogurt, 1 tablespoon lemon juice, 1 clove garlic (minced), 1 tablespoon chopped fresh dill, salt, pepper
- UK: 1 cucumber (seeded and grated), 240ml Greek yogurt, 1 tablespoon lemon juice, 1 clove garlic (minced), 1 tablespoon chopped fresh dill, salt, pepper

Instructions:

1. Grate cucumber and squeeze out excess moisture using a clean kitchen towel.
2. In a bowl, combine grated cucumber, Greek yogurt, lemon juice, minced garlic, chopped fresh dill, salt, and pepper.
3. Mix well and refrigerate for at least 30 minutes before serving.

Nutritional Info: Calories: 70 | Fat: 1g | Carbs: 8g | Protein: 8g

Mango Salsa

Prep: 10 mins | Cook: 0 mins | Makes: 2 cups

Ingredients:

- US: 2 ripe mangoes (diced), 1/2 red onion (finely chopped), 1 red bell pepper (diced), 1 jalapeño (seeded and minced), 1/4 cup chopped fresh cilantro, 2 tablespoons lime juice, salt, pepper
- UK: 2 ripe mangoes (diced), 1/2 red onion (finely chopped), 1 red bell pepper (diced), 1 jalapeño (seeded and minced), 1/4 cup chopped fresh cilantro, 2 tablespoons lime juice, salt, pepper

Instructions:

1. In a bowl, combine diced mangoes, chopped red onion, diced red bell pepper, minced jalapeño, chopped fresh cilantro, lime juice, salt, and pepper.
2. Mix well and refrigerate for at least 15 minutes before serving.

Nutritional Info: Calories: 45 | Fat: 0g | Carbs: 12g | Protein: 1g

Honey Mustard Dressing

Prep: 5 mins | Cook: 0 mins | Makes: 1/2 cup

Ingredients:

- US: 60ml Dijon mustard, 2 tablespoons honey, 2 tablespoons apple cider vinegar, 60ml olive oil, salt, pepper
- UK: 60ml Dijon mustard, 2 tablespoons honey, 2 tablespoons apple cider vinegar, 60ml olive oil, salt, pepper

Instructions:

1. In a bowl, whisk together Dijon mustard, honey, apple cider vinegar, olive oil, salt, and pepper until smooth.
2. Adjust seasoning to taste.
3. Serve immediately or refrigerate until ready to use.

Nutritional Info: Calories: 80 | Fat: 7g | Carbs: 5g | Protein: 0g

Garlic Aioli

Prep: 5 mins | Cook: 0 mins | Makes: 1/2 cup

Ingredients:

- US: 1/2 cup mayonnaise, 1 clove garlic (minced), 1 tablespoon lemon juice, salt, pepper
- UK: 120ml mayonnaise, 1 clove garlic (minced), 1 tablespoon lemon juice, salt, pepper

Instructions:

1. In a bowl, mix mayonnaise, minced garlic, lemon juice, salt, and pepper until well combined.
2. Adjust seasoning to taste.
3. Refrigerate for at least 30 minutes before serving to allow the flavors to meld.

Nutritional Info: Calories: 800 | Fat: 88g | Carbs: 2g | Protein: 1g

Chimichurri Sauce

Prep: 10 mins | Cook: 0 mins | Makes: 1 cup

Ingredients:

- US: 1 cup fresh parsley, 3 cloves garlic (minced), 2 tablespoons fresh oregano, 2 tablespoons red wine vinegar, 120ml olive oil, salt, pepper, red pepper flakes (optional)
- UK: 1 cup fresh parsley, 3 cloves garlic (minced), 2 tablespoons fresh oregano, 2 tablespoons red wine vinegar, 120ml olive oil, salt, pepper, red pepper flakes (optional)

Instructions:

1. In a food processor, combine fresh parsley, minced garlic, fresh oregano, red wine vinegar, olive oil, salt, pepper, and red pepper flakes if using.
2. Pulse until well blended but still slightly chunky.
3. Taste and adjust seasoning if necessary.
4. Transfer to a jar and refrigerate until ready to use.

Nutritional Info: Calories: 120 | Fat: 14g | Carbs: 2g | Protein: 1g

Ranch Dressing

Prep: 5 mins | Cook: 0 mins | Makes: 1 cup

Ingredients:

- US: 1/2 cup mayonnaise, 1/2 cup sour cream, 1/4 cup milk, 1 teaspoon dried parsley, 1/2 teaspoon dried dill, 1/2 teaspoon garlic powder, 1/2 teaspoon onion powder, salt, pepper
- UK: 120ml mayonnaise, 120ml sour cream, 60ml milk, 1 teaspoon dried parsley, 1/2 teaspoon dried dill, 1/2 teaspoon garlic powder, 1/2 teaspoon onion powder, salt, pepper

Instructions:

1. In a bowl, whisk together mayonnaise, sour cream, milk, dried parsley, dried dill, garlic powder, onion powder, salt, and pepper until smooth.
2. Adjust seasoning to taste.
3. Refrigerate for at least 30 minutes before serving.

Nutritional Info: Calories: 120 | Fat: 12g | Carbs: 2g | Protein: 1g

Pesto Sauce

Prep: 10 mins | Cook: 0 mins | Makes: 1 cup

Ingredients:

- US: 2 cups fresh basil leaves, 2 cloves garlic, 1/4 cup pine nuts, 1/2 cup grated Parmesan cheese, 120ml olive oil, salt, pepper
- UK: 50g fresh basil leaves, 2 cloves garlic, 30g pine nuts, 50g grated Parmesan cheese, 120ml olive oil, salt, pepper

Instructions:

1. In a food processor, combine basil leaves, garlic, pine nuts, and Parmesan cheese.
2. Pulse until finely chopped.
3. With the processor running, gradually add olive oil until smooth.
4. Season with salt and pepper to taste.
5. Store in a sealed container in the refrigerator.

Nutritional Info: Calories: 80 | Fat: 8g | Carbs: 1g | Protein: 2g

Sweet and Sour Sauce

Prep: 5 mins | Cook: 10 mins | Makes: 1 cup

Ingredients:

- US: 120ml pineapple juice, 60ml rice vinegar, 60ml ketchup, 3 tablespoons brown sugar, 1 tablespoon soy sauce, 1 tablespoon cornstarch, 60ml water
- UK: 120ml pineapple juice, 60ml rice vinegar, 60ml ketchup, 3 tablespoons brown sugar, 1 tablespoon soy sauce, 1 tablespoon cornstarch, 60ml water

Instructions:

1. In a small saucepan, combine pineapple juice, rice vinegar, ketchup, brown sugar, and soy sauce.
2. In a separate bowl, mix cornstarch and water until smooth.
3. Add cornstarch mixture to the saucepan and whisk to combine.
4. Bring to a boil, then reduce heat and simmer for 57 minutes, or until thickened.
5. Allow to cool before serving.

Nutritional Info: Calories: 30 | Fat: 0g | Carbs: 8g | Protein: 0g

CONCLUSION

Congratulations on completing the culinary journey through the Ninja Foodi Smart-Lid Cookbook! Throughout this cookbook, we've explored a variety of mouthwatering recipes designed to elevate your cooking experience using the innovative features of the Ninja Foodi Smart-Lid. From hearty main courses to delightful snacks and appetizers, each recipe has been carefully crafted to deliver convenience, flavor, and satisfaction to your table.

As you've discovered, the Ninja Foodi Smart-Lid is more than just a kitchen appliance; it's a versatile cooking companion that streamlines meal preparation while ensuring delicious results every time. Whether you're a busy parent looking for quick weekday dinners, a seasoned chef seeking creative inspiration, or someone simply passionate about good food, the Ninja Foodi Smart-Lid offers a range of functions to suit your culinary needs.

In this cookbook, we've covered a diverse range of recipes spanning different cuisines, cooking styles, and occasions. From succulent mains like Beef Stew and Lemon Herb Roast Chicken to tempting appetizers like Buffalo Chicken Dip and Stuffed Mushroom Caps, there's something to tantalize every palate. The Ninja Foodi Smart-Lid's functions, including Pressure Cook, Air Crisp, Bake, and more, have been expertly utilized to bring out the best in each dish, ensuring optimal flavor and texture with minimal effort.

One of the key highlights of the Ninja Foodi Smart-Lid Cookbook is its emphasis on convenience without compromising on taste. With features like Pressure Cook for speedy cooking, Air Crisp for achieving crispy textures without excess oil, and Bake for perfect oven-like results, you can whip up restaurant-quality meals right in your own kitchen. Whether you're cooking for a crowd or preparing a cozy meal for two, the Ninja Foodi Smart-Lid simplifies the cooking process, allowing you to spend less time in the kitchen and more time enjoying delicious food with loved ones.

Furthermore, this cookbook embraces a balanced approach to cooking, offering a mix of indulgent treats and healthier options to suit every dietary preference. Whether you're craving cheesy Pretzel Bites with Beer Cheese or opting for lighter fare like Caprese Skewers, each recipe has been thoughtfully crafted to provide both nourishment and enjoyment. With the Ninja Foodi Smart-Lid, you have the flexibility to explore a wide range of ingredients and flavors, empowering you to customize meals to your liking while maintaining control over portion sizes and nutritional content.

In addition to its culinary prowess, the Ninja Foodi Smart-Lid Cookbook also serves as a source of inspiration and education for home cooks of all skill levels. Each recipe is accompanied by clear, concise instructions presented in a casual, approachable manner, making it easy for even novice cooks to follow along. Whether you're learning new techniques like pressure cooking or experimenting with flavor combinations, this cookbook provides the guidance and support you need to succeed in the kitchen.

As you continue your culinary journey with the Ninja Foodi Smart-Lid, don't be afraid to get creative and adapt the recipes to suit your tastes and preferences. Feel free to swap ingredients, adjust seasonings, or experiment with different cooking methods to make each dish your own. After all, cooking is as much about exploration and discovery as it is about nourishment and sustenance.

In closing, I hope this cookbook has inspired you to unleash your inner chef and embrace the possibilities of cooking with the Ninja Foodi Smart-Lid. Whether you're cooking for yourself, your family, or your friends, may each meal be a celebration of good food, good company, and good times. Happy cooking!

Printed in Great Britain
by Amazon

53277370R00040

PREAMBLE AND CREDITS

This book is intended for children from 10 years old (depending on the reading level).

Astronomical concepts have sometimes been deliberately simplified, in order to be adapted to the age of the readers. In the same way, measurements of temperature, distance, size, and speed are systematically written in several scales of units, in order to adapt to all children, whatever their origins and places of life.

Finally, some terms have been grouped under a single name. For example, the term "astronomer" is regularly used in this book, and groups together all the specialties of the astronomy professions. The same goes for the term "astronaut", which is used generically and includes the terms "astronaut, spationaut, cosmonaut, and taikonaut".

IMAGE CREDIT: Freepik.com

Thanks to CATALYSTUFF, MACROVECTOR, UPKLYAK, BRGFX, KJPARJETER, VADIMSADOVSKI and other Freepik.com contributors.

CONTENTS

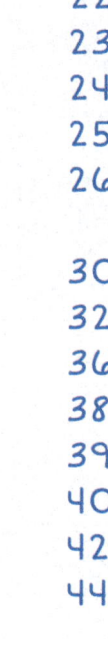

CONTENTS

INTRODUCTION

ASTRONOMY ?

Astronomy, the study and observation of the celestial objects, is certainly the oldest of the sciences.

Nowadays, we know many things about the universe.

Our scientific knowledge allows us to understand many astronomical phenomena.
We have observation satellites, and we send men into space and robots to Mars.

But it is important to know that the first men were already observing the sky, as attested by the discovery of 32,000 year old engraved bones, whose symbols represent the lunar movements.

For a very long time, man believed that the Earth was flat and that it was the center of the universe.

2000 years before our era, the Babylonians had already observed 5 different celestial objects in the sky. Historians and astronomers believe that they had discovered Mercury, Mars, Venus, Saturn and Jupiter.

600 years before Christ, the Greeks, thanks to various observations, had concluded that the Earth was round.

The ancient civilizations of South America (first the Mayans, then the Aztecs and the Incas) had created very precise calendars, based on their astronomical observations.

In 1543, the Polish astronomer Nicolaus Copernicus demonstrated that the Earth revolved around the sun (and not the other way around, as was thought at the time).

At the beginning of the 17th century, Johannes Kepler (German astronomer), demonstrated the elliptical motion of the planets, and Galileo (Italian scientist) considerably improved the astronomical observation glasses.

In 1687, Isaac Newton, an English scientist, developed the laws of universal gravitation.

The progress of science and technology has then allowed us to considerably improve our astronomical knowledge, and to have a better understanding of the Universe.

The Mpumalanga Circle (also called Adam's calendar), discovered in 2003 in South Africa, is the oldest known solar calendar. Formed by various monoliths (i.e. large stones), it would date from at least 75 000 years.

The Circle of Goseck, located in Germany, is considered as one of the very first astronomical observatories.
Also discovered in 2003, this observatory of more than 7000 years old was certainly intended for agriculture, in order to know with precision the solar cycles.

SPACE

When we look at the stars in the sky, we think that the space (between the stars) is empty. In reality, even though we can't see anything, space is filled with dust, particles, and gas.

However, this matter has a low density, and that is why we consider that space is empty. The density is the quantity of matter contained in a volume. The more this quantity is important, the more the density is important (and conversely).

In space, things don't work like on Earth.

For example, it is impossible to breathe in space, because there is no oxygen.

Another example, sounds cannot propagate in space. Sound is a mechanical wave (like a vibration) that propagates by deforming and compressing matter. On Earth, a sound propagates in a gaseous matter (like air), liquid matter (like water) or solid matter (like a wall).

In space, there is not enough matter for this wave to propagate.

As for light, it is a little more complicated: Light is an electromagnetic wave (unlike sound which is a mechanical wave), and it does not need matter to propagate. However, it needs matter to be visible.

On Earth, when it is daytime (thanks to the sun's light rays), we see light, because it reflects on our atmosphere (mainly made of nitrogen, oxygen, and water vapor), on objects (made of various matter), and even on us (and we are made of matter too).

In space, the light (produced for example by a star) will propagate in the vacuum. It will not be able to reflect on the matter. This is why space remains black.

The light (and especially its speed) plays a very important role in the study of space.

The universe is immense, and nobody knows its exact size (perhaps it is infinite?). The distances between galaxies, planets or stars are really gigantic.

So, to calculate these distances, astronomers use a specific unit: the light-year.

Light moves very fast. It is, in fact, the fastest known speed. This speed is 300 000 kilometers per second (186 000 Miles per second).

A light-year is therefore the distance that light travels in one year, that is to say 9500 billion kilometers (5900 billion Miles).

The light from the sun takes 8 minutes to reach the Earth. This means that the light that we perceive now left the sun 8 minutes ago.
But, on the scale of the universe, the sun is very close to our planet. The stars we see at night are much farther away. Some of them are more than 8000 light years away from our planet! This means that the light from these stars, which we see today, took 8000 years to reach us.

GRAVITY

Gravity (also called gravitation, force of gravity or gravitational force) is the attraction between 2 bodies (i.e. between 2 elements made of matter, living or not). These elements attract each other, like magnets, more or less strongly depending on their mass (i.e. the quantity of matter that composes them).

This is why if we throw a ball in the air, it falls back to the ground. The Earth has a much greater mass than a ball. All the objects around us are held on the surface of the Earth by the force of gravity.

As the distance between objects increases, the force of gravity decreases. If an object moves far enough away from the Earth, it "floats" in space. The distance it moves away will depend mainly on the mass of the object.

Gravitation is not only a terrestrial phenomenon, and applies to the whole universe. It is also the gravitation that allows the moon to rotate around the Earth. The Earth attracts the moon by its gravitational force.

But why doesn't the moon crash into the Earth?
The gravitational force of the Earth causes an attraction on the moon, but the moon turns around the Earth because it has its own speed. This movement is the result of the birth of the moon (which we will see later).
It is the balance between the speed of movement of the moon and the force of gravitation that allows the moon to remain at a certain distance from the earth, without colliding with it. If the speed of the moon were to increase sharply, the gravitational force could no longer hold it and it would fly off into space. Conversely, if its speed decreased, the gravitational force would attract the moon towards the Earth and the two celestial objects would eventually collide.

To understand gravitation on the scale of the universe, let's do a little experiment:

Let's take a ball (or another small round object) and attach a string.

Let's take the string in our hand and make the ball turn.

The ball is now spinning around our hand in the same way that the moon is spinning around the Earth. The string represents the gravitational force.

If we spin the ball faster and faster, we will feel more and more tension on the string.

If we let go of the string, the ball is thrown away. This is what would happen if the moon spun so fast that the gravitational force of the Earth could no longer hold it.

If we slow down the movement of the ball, its trajectory will become random and it will eventually stop. Without motion, only the gravitational force will act on the ball.

THE BIG BANG

Most astronomers believe that the universe, as we know it today, was created by a "big bang".

This theory was born in the early 20th century. Thanks to the work of Vesto Slipher and Edwin Hubble (American astronomers), scientists discovered that galaxies are moving away from each other and concluded that the universe is expanding. For his part, Albert Einstein published the theory of general relativity, which describes the gravitational attraction.

Recent observations confirm this theory of the Big Bang, which is now validated by the majority of scientists.

Almost 14 billion years ago, the entire universe was contained in a very small mass, probably the size of a football. This mass was very dense, and very hot (billions of degrees).

Then, for some unknown reason, this mass suddenly "burst", with an unimaginable power.

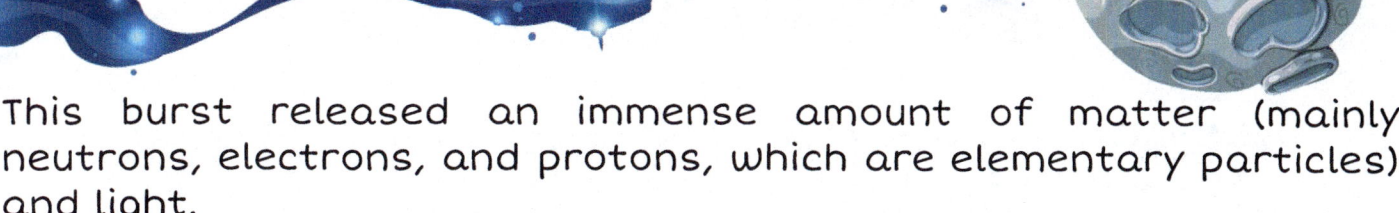

This burst released an immense amount of matter (mainly neutrons, electrons, and protons, which are elementary particles) and light.

A few minutes later, under the effect of the drop in temperature, the neutrons and protons began to come together to form simple atomic nuclei (hydrogen, helium, lithium).

380,000 years later, the temperature being much cooler (a few thousand degrees), electrons were able to bind to atomic nuclei and form the first atoms.

This association allowed light to circulate freely. Until this period, the light particles were blocked by this "fog" of electrons.

About 150 million years after the Big Bang, the particles of matter grouped in the form of clouds, stuck together, mainly under the effect of gravitation. These agglomerated particles gave birth to the first stars, and allowed the fusion of atomic nuclei and the creation of new elements (such as carbon, nitrogen, or oxygen).

Today, the average temperature of the universe is 2.7 Kelvin (-271 degrees Celsius / -456 degrees Fahrenheit).

STARS

STARS

A star is a celestial object that emits its own light.

We can observe thousands of them from Earth, but we cannot see them all. Some are so far away that we cannot see them.

No one knows exactly how many stars there are in the universe, but there are billions of billions.

Stars do not stand still in space. They move and turn on themselves (this is called rotation). But because they are so far away from us, their movements are imperceptible.

The first stars were formed about 400 million years after the Big Bang.

How is a star formed?

A huge cloud of matter (mainly hydrogen but also other particles) begins to condense under the effect of gravitation. This concentration of matter causes a rotation, and the cloud of particles starts to rotate faster and faster. The hydrogen atoms, more and more concentrated, begin to fuse together, under the effect of the pressure. This fusion transforms the hydrogen atoms into helium atoms, and causes a great quantity of heat and light. A star is born.

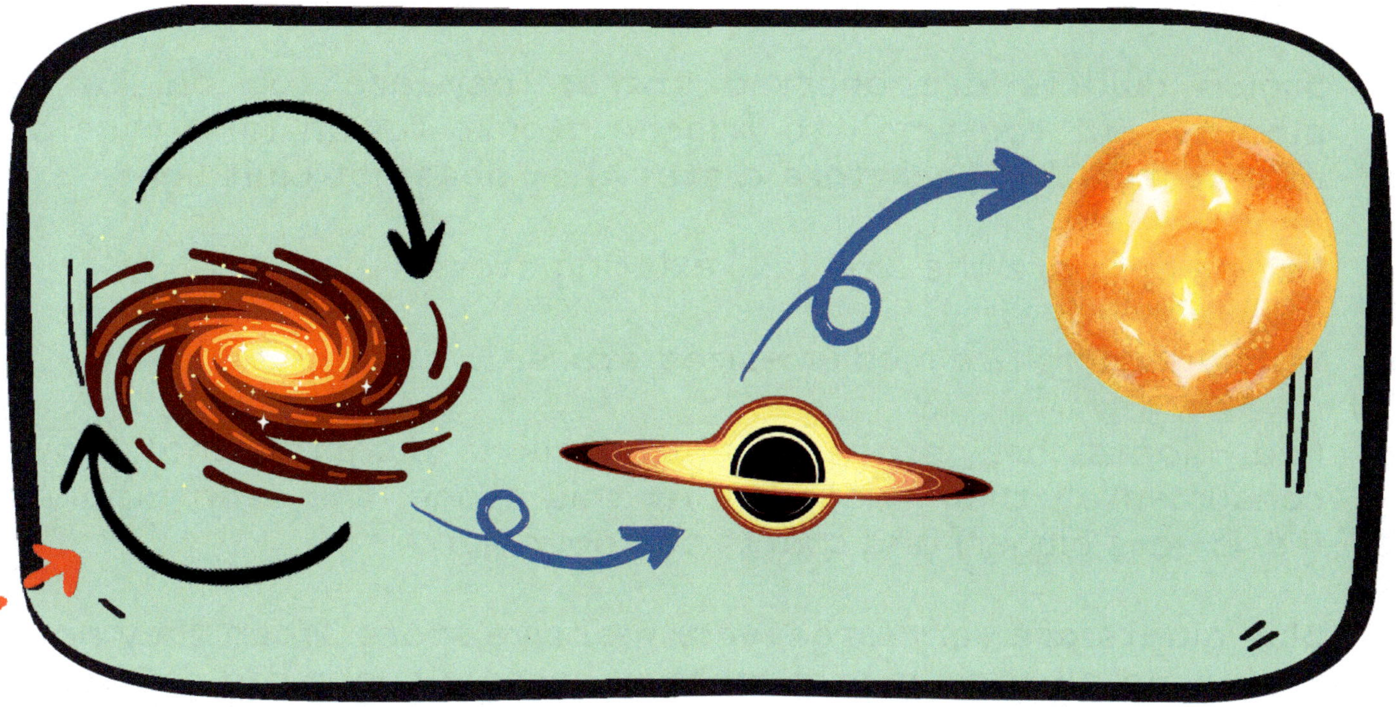

In simple terms, a star is a compact ball of matter (mainly gas) in fusion.

Atomic fusion (also called nuclear fusion) also allows the creation of new atoms: Fusion transforms hydrogen atoms into helium atoms, which in turn (and under increasing pressure) will transform into carbon and oxygen atoms, which will then transform into calcium, sodium, magnesium, potassium, and even iron atoms.

There are several categories of stars. Generally, astronomers classify them according to their size, their mass, their density (i.e. the amount of matter in relation to their size), and their life stage.

- Brown dwarfs are aborted stars. They are too big to be planets, but too small to trigger atomic fusion (and thus be real stars). It is therefore a star that does not emit light.

- Red dwarfs are the smallest existing stars.

- Yellow dwarfs are medium-sized stars.

- Red giants are stars (usually yellow dwarfs) that have consumed all their hydrogen. At this stage, the star expands (i.e. it gets bigger) and starts to cool down.

- Blue giants are very large, very massive stars. When they have consumed all their hydrogen, they become super red giants. In general, they end up exploding in supernova.

- Neutron stars are the remains of the core (also called the nucleus) of a very large star (super red giant) after its explosion.

- White dwarfs are dead stars, meaning that they no longer burn matter. When they are completely cooled, they become black dwarfs.

The color of the light emitted by a star depends on its temperature. Red stars are the coldest stars (less than 4000° Celsius or 7100° Fahrenheit), yellow stars have a temperature of about 6000° Celsius (10800° Fahrenheit), and blue stars have a temperature of over 7000° Celsius (12500° Fahrenheit).

The oldest known star is called Methuselah (in reference to the character of the same name in the Bible, who would have lived more than 900 years). The age of this star is estimated at 13.2 billion years.

And the closest star to us?
It is the sun! The sun is a star. It produces its own light.

The closest star to Earth, apart from the sun, is called Proxima Centauri. It is the closest, but it is still 4.2 light years away.

From Earth, there are about 7000 stars visible to the naked eye. But it is sometimes difficult to see some of them, because of clouds for example, but also because of artificial lighting that prevents us from distinguishing the less bright stars.

THE DEATH OF A STAR

Stars live until they run out of energy (that is, until they have burned all their gas). Some stars shine for billions of years, and others for only a few million years.

Then, one day, they die.

Generally, the smallest stars will release various elements into space (in the form of particles and gas), then cool down and become white dwarfs and then black dwarfs. They are very dense and composed of residual solid matter.

The largest stars (super red giants) explode and release an immense amount of energy and matter into space. This phenomenon is called a supernova.

By exploding, a supernova will create new atoms, heavier than iron, such as tin, lead, silver and gold.

Observing the explosion of a supernova is rare.
There are accounts that a very bright star was observed in 1006. It was visible from parts of Asia and Arabia. Today, we know that it was a supernova located 7000 light years from Earth.
The last observation of a supernova from Earth occurred in 1604. Scientists estimate that it was 20,000 light years from Earth.

The amount of matter released into space at the time of the death of a star will then allow new stars to be created.

22

STARDUST

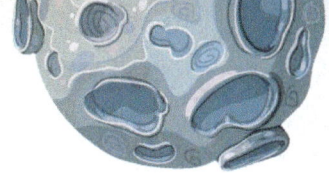

Everything around us is composed of atoms: the sky, the earth, water, objects, living beings (plants and animals)...

Our body is obviously also composed of atoms, mainly carbon, hydrogen, nitrogen, oxygen, calcium, and phosphorus.

Hydrogen was created by the Big Bang and is the main component of stars. The other elements (thus the other atoms) are created within the stars themselves, thanks to fusion.

Then a star dies and releases into space the immense quantity of atoms that it has created.

Sometimes, some of the atoms will join together and form molecules, like water (composed of oxygen and hydrogen).

This means that all the matter that surrounds us comes from atoms created by the stars, such as the oxygen we breathe, the water we drink, our fork (iron, aluminum), our jewelry (gold, silver...)...

The atoms that make up our bodies were also created "in the stars", millions and millions of years ago.

There is stardust in our body!

SHOOTING STARS

We have all seen a shooting star. However, a shooting star is not a star. It is in fact a meteor!

A meteor is a small rock that enters the Earth's atmosphere (attracted by the Earth because of the gravitational force).

Its speed is very high and can reach 250 000 km/h (155000 mph). The friction of the air on the surface of the meteor then causes a very strong heat, and the meteor ignites.

Most of the time, this phenomenon lasts barely a second.

When we see a shooting star, it is actually a small stone that burns.

Usually, a meteor burns up completely in the atmosphere. But sometimes a small piece manages to fall to Earth. This is called a meteorite.

A meteorite is a small stone from space. It can be composed of rock, but also of metal.

But where do meteors come from?

A meteor is, most of the time, a debris of asteroid or comet.

ASTEROIDS AND COMETS

Often, asteroids and comets are themselves debris or remnants of planets (some asteroids are even considered as planet embryos).

Asteroids are composed mainly of rocks, metals, and sometimes ice. They are in orbit around a star (i.e. they revolve around a star).

They are usually a few tens of meters long, but some can be more than 500 kilometers (310 Miles) long.

Comets are composed primarily of ice, frozen gas, and some clumps of rock. Like asteroids, comets orbit a star, but at a greater distance.

When a comet gets close to a star, under the effect of heat, it starts to melt. Two "tails" appear behind it: a yellow one, made of dust, and a blue one, made of gas.

CONSTELLATIONS

A constellation is the name given to a group of stars observable from Earth.

It is a human invention. In ancient times, astronomers began to draw maps of the sky. In order to find their way around, they invented "shapes" by linking certain stars together. In fact, many constellations are named after fantastic animals or characters from Greek mythology.

In ancient times, constellations were different in different countries and cultures. For example, the Chinese did not "invent" the same constellations as the Greeks.

At the beginning of the 20th century, scientists agreed on 88 constellations, including the 12 constellations of the zodiac.

On Earth, we have the impression that the stars of a constellation are very close, but in reality, they are very distant from each other.

It is also important to know that we do not all see the same stars and constellations: If we live in the northern hemisphere (the part between the equator and the north pole), we will not see the same constellations as those who live in the southern hemisphere (the part between the equator and the south pole), and conversely.

A map of the sky, with the main constellations, can be found on the next page.

IMPORTANT: Everything moves in space, which means that the stars and constellations are not always in the same place. Depending on the season and the time of day, the constellations will be out of place and will not have the exact location defined on the map.

NORTHERN
HEMISPHERE

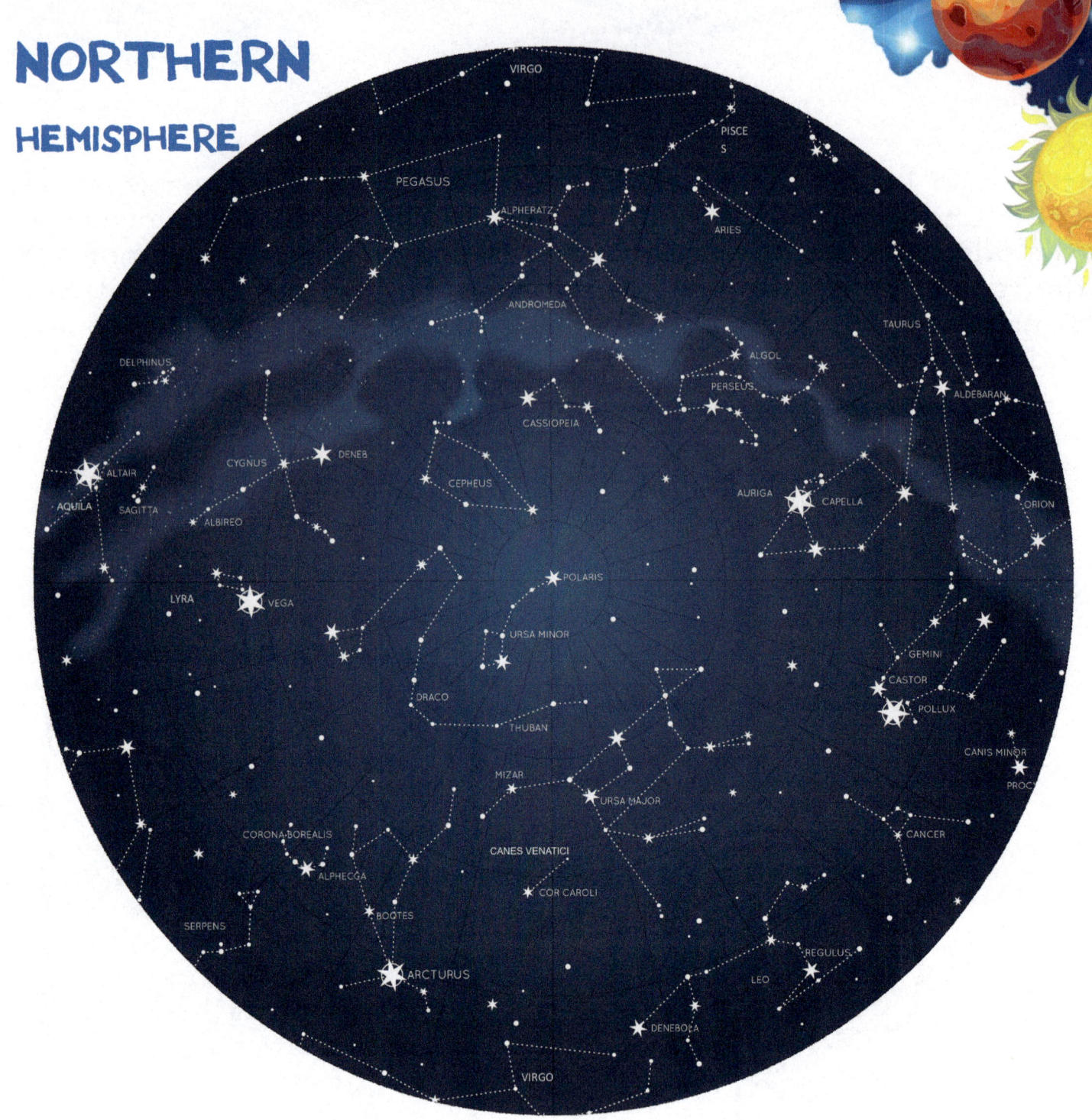

Aquila	Eagle	Sagitta	Arrow
Andromeda	Princess of Ethiopia	Gemini	Twins
Aries	Ram	Ursa major	Big bear
Bootes	Herdsman	Leo	Lion
Cancer	Crab	Lyra	Lyre
Cassiopeia	Cassiopée	Orion	Orion the hunter
Cepheus	Céphée	Pegasus	Pegasus the winged horse
Canes venatici	Hunting dogs	Perseus	Perseus
Auriga	Charioteer	Canis Minor	Little dog
Corona borealis	Northern crown	Ursa minor	Little bear
Cygnus	Swan	Taurus	Bull
Delphinus	Porpoise	Virgo	Virgin
Draco	Dragon		

The names of the constellations are written in Latin on the map and then translated (in blue).

SOUTHERN
HEMISPHERE

Libra	Balance	**Lepus**	Hare	**Triangulum aus.**	Southern triangle
Cetus	Whale	**Lupus**	Wolf	**Aquarius**	Water bearer
Capricornus	Sea goat	**Musca**	Fly	**Vela**	Boat sail
Carina	Boat keel	**Ophiuchus**	Holder of serpent		
Centaurus	Centaur	**Pavo**	Peacock		
Columba	Dove	**Phoenix**	Phoenix		
Corvus	Crow	**Piscis austrinus**	Southern fish		
Crux	Cross	**Pisces**	Fishes		
Eridanus	River	**Puppis**	Boat stern		
Canis major	Big dog	**Sagittarius**	Archer		
Grus	Crane	**Scorpius**	Scorpion		
Hydra	Sea serpent	**Serpens**	Serpent		
Hydrus	Water snake	**Tucana**	Toucan		

The names of the constellations are written in Latin on the map and then translated (in blue).

PLANETS

PLANETS

A planet is a celestial object that orbits a star (i.e. it revolves around it).

Unlike stars, planets do not emit light.

How are planets formed?
When a star is formed, a large amount of matter remains around it. This matter (gas, rock, metals...) flattens out to form a disk (or rather a cloud in the shape of a disk), which rotates around the star.
Within this cloud, a certain amount of gas and solid matter (rock for example) condenses under the effect of gravitation, and begins to turn on itself (a bit like a tornado). The particles of matter start to stick to each other, forming a cluster that gets bigger and bigger. When this cluster reaches a sufficient mass, it becomes a planet.

Why do planets revolve around stars?
Again, it's a matter of gravitation.
A star is much larger than a planet, and its mass (the amount of matter that makes it up) is much greater. When the star is formed, it causes a rotation of particles around it. These particles will later form planets, which will continue to rotate around the star. This phenomenon is called revolution.

A planet revolves around a star following a circular path called the orbit.

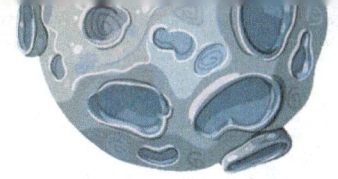

A planet rotates around a star, but it also turns on itself. This phenomenon, called rotation, is due to its birth: As we have just seen, the formation of a planet results from the agglomeration of particles within a cloud rotating on itself. When all the matter is agglomerated, it continues its rotation, by effect of inertia (i.e. it keeps its speed of movement). And as space is empty, nothing slows down this movement. The planet will therefore continue its rotation.

Moreover, the stars, which are formed in almost the same way as the planets, also turn on themselves.

But then, if stars and planets are formed in the same way, why do stars shine and planets do not?
This difference is mainly explained by two elements: Composition and mass.
A star is formed essentially from hydrogen (which is a gas).
Some planets are formed from rocks and metals, but there are planets formed from gases, including hydrogen. The composition is not enough to explain the difference between a planet and a star.
In fact, a star is much larger than a planet. It therefore contains much more matter, and it is this quantity of matter that will condense and cause (under the effect of gravitation) a strong heat and a nuclear reaction (i.e. the transformation of atoms). To make it simple, this reaction ignites the star.

To simplify, a star burns, and a planet does not burn.

The planets have a core located in their center (like the core of a peach).
It is a mass of very dense matter, often composed of metals (such as iron), and sometimes of rocks.

There are 2 categories of planets:

Telluric planets (also called rocky planets or terrestrial planets) are planets composed of hard material (like rock for example) and usually quite small. Most of the time, they have a core of solid or molten material.
Our planet, the Earth, is a telluric planet.

Gaseous planets are mainly composed of gas. They too have a core, but the rest of their mass is composed mainly of hydrogen and helium (i.e. gas). In other words, these planets have no solid surface and it would be impossible to walk on them.
Gaseous planets are larger than telluric planets.

Why are planets round?

The planets (and the stars) are all spherical. This is explained, once again, by gravitation: When a cluster of matter becomes large enough, the gravitational force increases. The matter is therefore attracted to the center of the planet. The spherical shape is precisely the shape that allows the matter to be as close as possible to its center.

So, naturally, planets and stars become round. The planets and stars have a sufficiently large mass to generate this phenomenon. Conversely, an asteroid, much smaller, is not subject to as much gravitational force. This is why asteroids are "potato" shaped.

STRUCTURE OF A PLANET

The telluric planets have almost all the same structure.

They have a core composed of metals (mostly iron).

Around this core is the mantle, which is composed of rock (often silicon, but sometimes carbon) and metals.

The outer part (the surface of the planet) is called the crust, and is composed of materials that vary from planet to planet. The crust of the Earth is composed of rocks but also of water.

Finally, most of the telluric planets have an atmosphere composed of gas, whose composition also varies from one planet to another.

1 Core

2 Mantle

3 Crust

4 Atmosphere

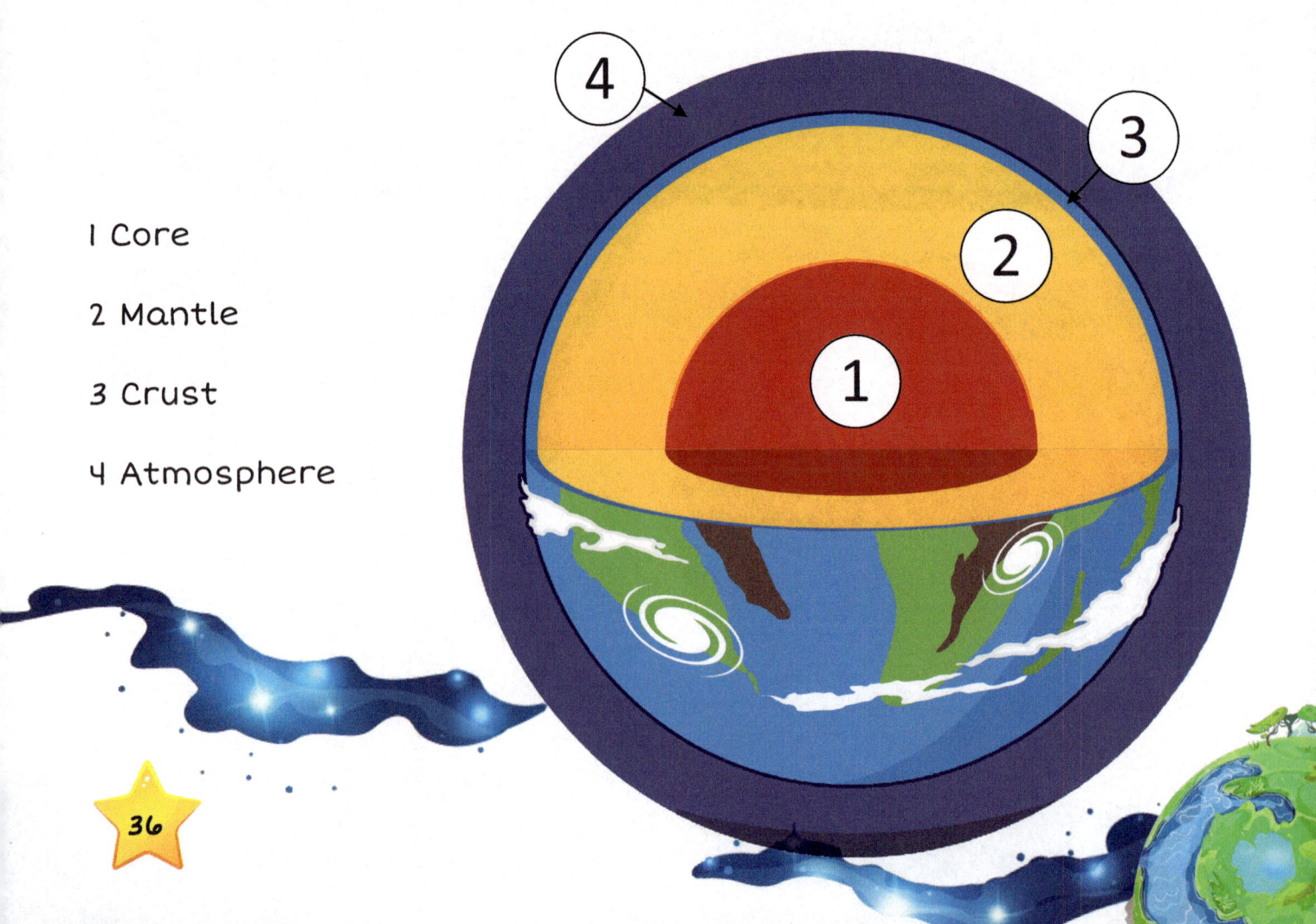

The gaseous planets are classified in 2 categories according to their structure.

The standard gas planets have a core composed of rock, more or less large, and an envelope composed of gas (usually hydrogen and helium, but also other types of gas in smaller quantities).

The giant ice planets (which are also gas planets) have a rocky core, a mantle composed of ice whose thickness varies according to the planets, and a gas envelope.

The gas planets do not have crusts.

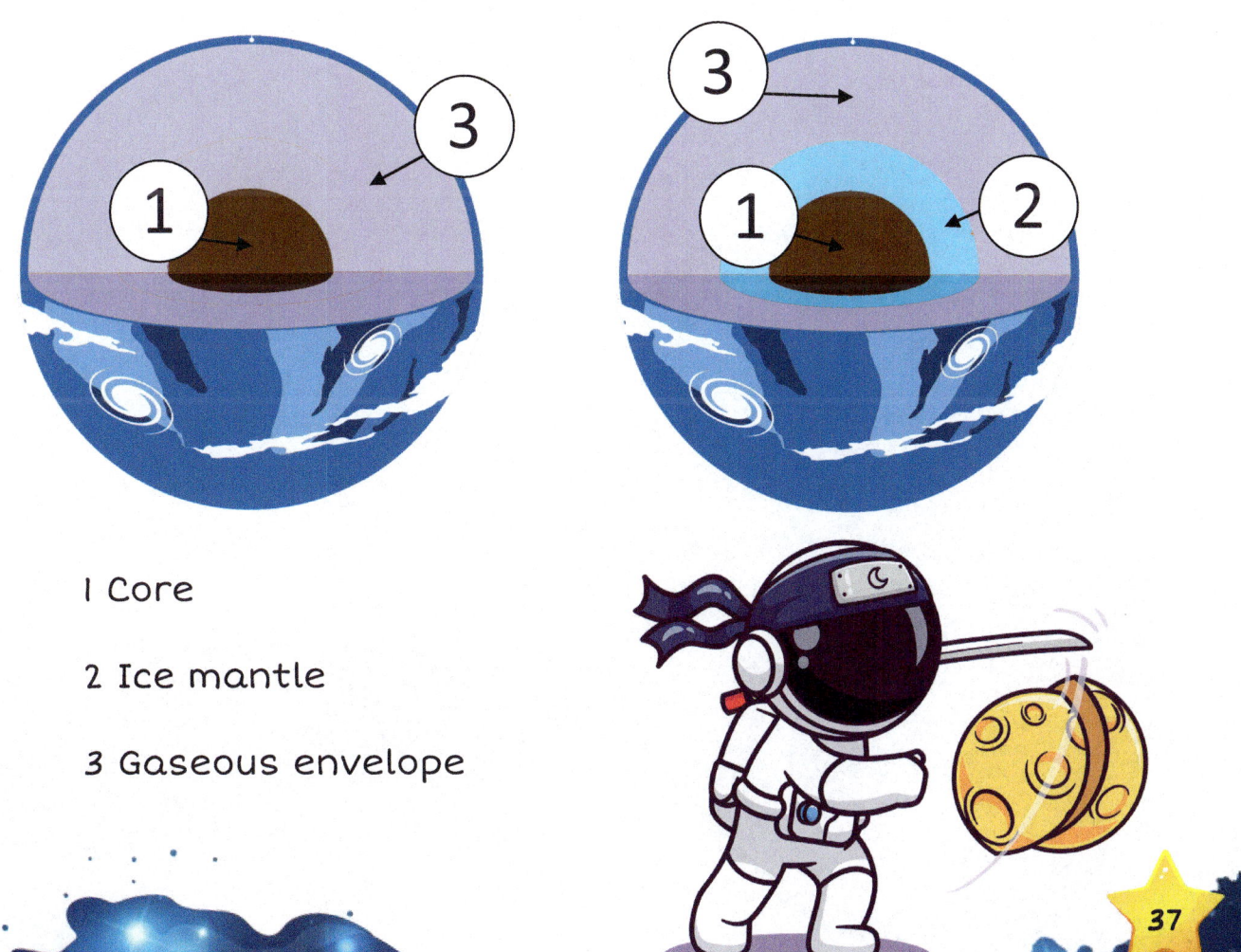

1 Core

2 Ice mantle

3 Gaseous envelope

ATMOSPHERE

The planetary atmosphere is the layer of gas enveloping a planet.

Most planets have one, but some do not.

The composition and thickness of the atmosphere are different from one planet to another. These differences depend on several parameters: the composition of the planet, the gravitation, the distance between the planet and its star...

On Earth, our atmosphere is largely composed of nitrogen and oxygen.

The atmosphere plays an important role in the life of a planet, and can for example regulate temperatures (greenhouse effect), filter certain radiations from the star (like ultraviolet rays), and participate in the appearance of life (which is the case on Earth).

For a human being, breathing on another planet is impossible, unless he lands on a planet whose atmosphere is identical to that of the Earth.

PLANETARY GEOGRAPHY

Here are some important definitions to talk about the planets:

The axis of rotation: The planets rotate on themselves around an axis of rotation. This axis is an imaginary line that passes through the center of the planet and through the poles.

The poles: These are the two points defined by the ends of the axis of rotation. The North Pole is located at the top of the planet, and the South Pole is located at the bottom.

The equator: This is an imaginary line running all the way around a planet, perpendicular to the axis of rotation and at equal distance from the poles, and dividing the planet into two equal hemispheres.

The diameter: A straight line connecting two points on the surface of a planet and passing through its center.

1 Axis of rotation

2 North pole

3 South Pole

4 Equator

5 Diameter

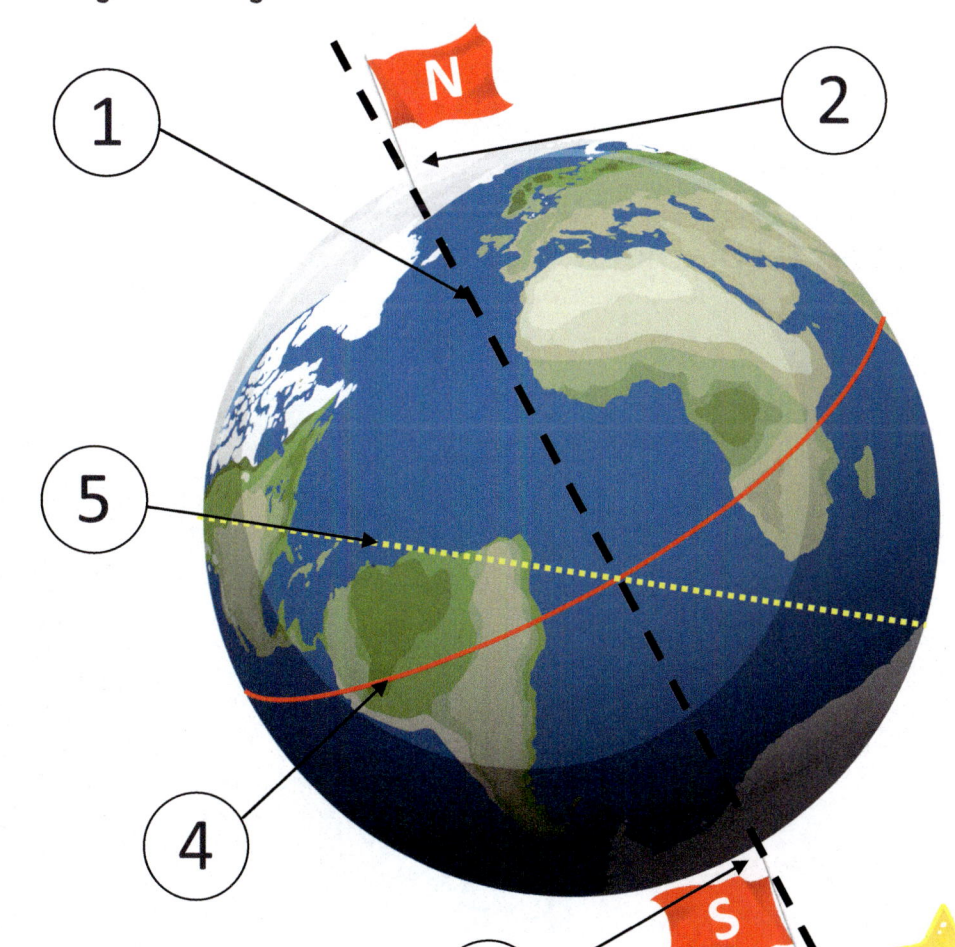

EXOPLANETS

Planets outside our solar system are called "exoplanets". Currently, astronomers have discovered more than 3000 of them.

However, they are very difficult to find and observe, because they are very far from our planet. It was not until the early 1990s that the first exoplanets were observed, thanks to modern technology.

Astronomers estimate that there are billions of planets in the universe. Some say that there are as many planets as there are grains of sand in the Sahara desert.

Moreover, there are incredible exoplanets:

The planet "55 Cancri E": Generally, the telluric planets are formed of silicate, that is to say a mixture of silicon (to make simple, sand) and metals. The planet "55 Cancri E" is composed largely of carbon, and the temperature at its surface is about 2500 degrees Celsius (4500 degrees Fahrenheit). It should be noted that carbon, when heated to a certain temperature and subjected to a very high pressure, turns into ... diamond!
This exoplanet is thus composed, for approximately one third of its mass, of diamond.

The planet "HD 189733 B" is also very hot (more than 1000 degrees Celsius on its surface, or 1800 degrees Fahrenheit). The surface of the planet is swept by winds of 7000 km/h (4350 mph) and its atmosphere is filled with particles of silicon that compact (under the effect of heat) to become small pieces of sharp glass. It rains glass on this planet!

The planet "Gliese 436 B" is a planet composed largely of water. Being very close to its star, its surface has a temperature of 250 degrees Celsius (480 degrees Fahrenheit). However, gravity is so strong on this planet that the water that evaporates instantly crystallizes and turns into a kind of hot ice.

SATELLITES

A natural satellite is a celestial object that revolves around a planet. Be careful not to confuse them with artificial satellites which are of human origin and which are used for telecommunications (television, radio...) and observation (weather forecasts, astronomical observations...).

Like the planets around the stars, the satellites have a circular trajectory around the planets (orbit), and they also turn on themselves.

The moon is the best known satellite, and especially the closest to us.

According to astronomers, satellites are formed in several ways:

By accretion: In the same way that a planet is formed around a star, a satellite can be formed from matter orbiting a planet. A cluster of matter forms and grows until it becomes a spherical celestial object.

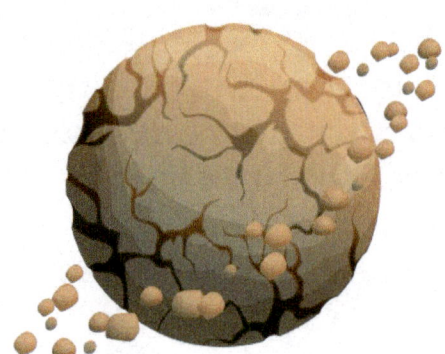

By capture: When asteroids get close enough to a planet, the gravitational force of the planet "captures" them. In other words, the asteroids are attracted to the planet by gravitational force. Then, the asteroids will stick together and form a satellite.

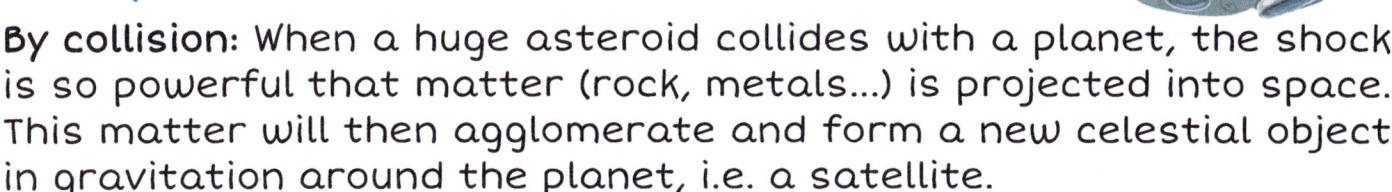

By collision: When a huge asteroid collides with a planet, the shock is so powerful that matter (rock, metals...) is projected into space. This matter will then agglomerate and form a new celestial object in gravitation around the planet, i.e. a satellite.

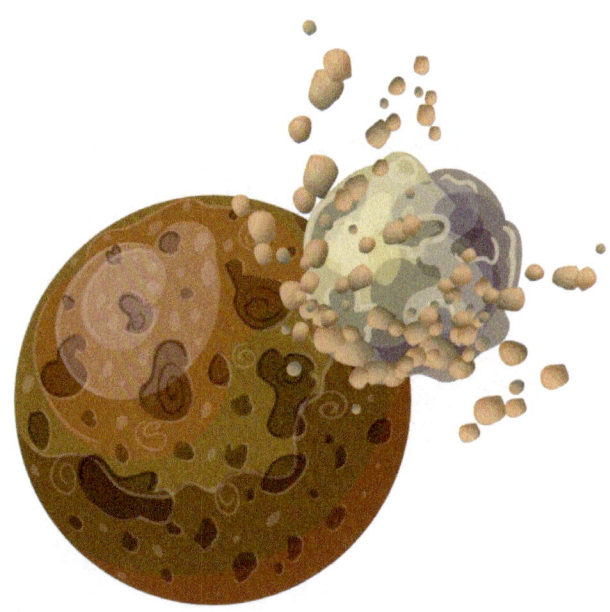

Some planets have rings around them. This is the case of Saturn for example. These rings are not satellites. They are composed of small pieces of material (rock, ice ...). Generally, this matter is a residue of the planet (i.e. a surplus of matter that has not agglomerated), or debris from asteroids or satellites.

DAY AND NIGHT

On all planets, there is day and night.

The planets all turn on themselves (this is called rotation). And all planets revolve around a star (this is called revolution).

The light coming from the star illuminates one half of the planet, while the other half receives no light.

As the planet rotates on itself, the part exposed to light changes constantly.

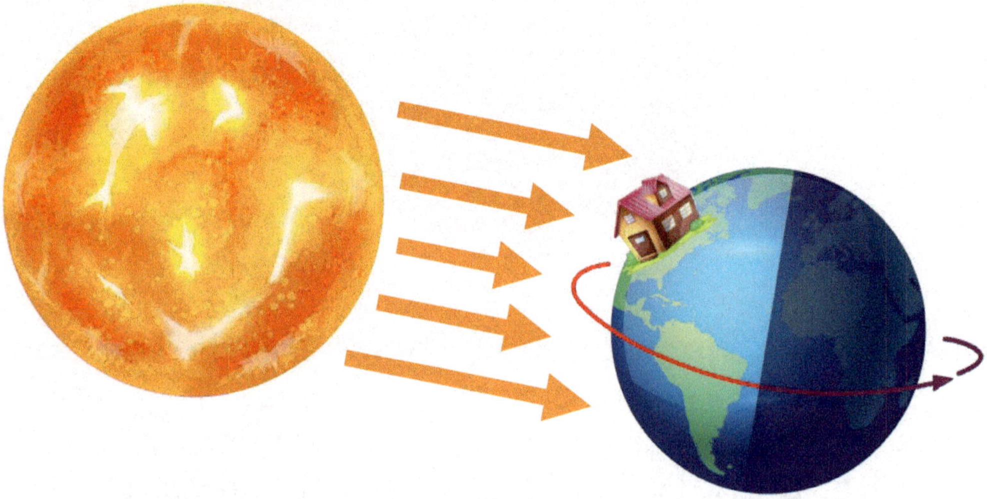

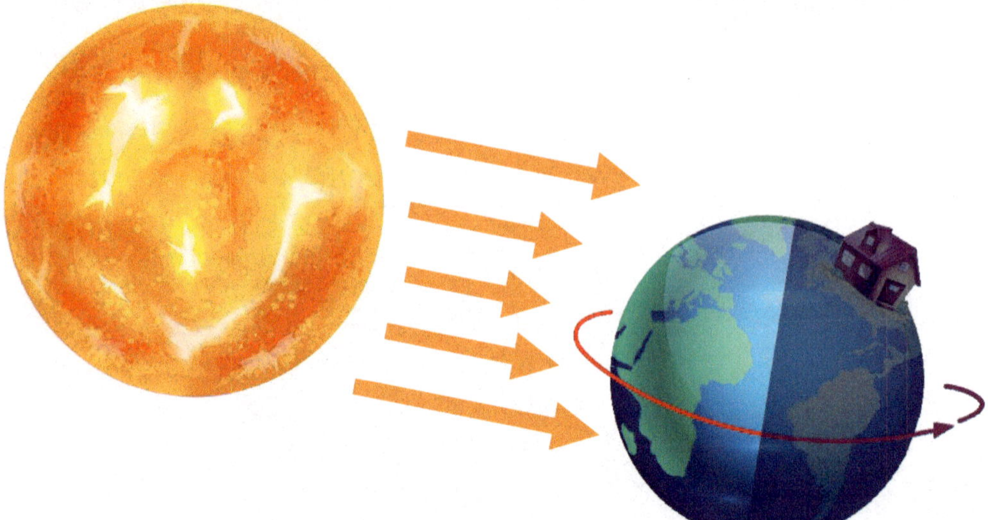

What is called a day (day + night) corresponds to a complete rotation of a planet.

On Earth, a day lasts 24 hours, that is to say that the Earth makes a complete turn on itself in 24 hours. During these 24 hours, day and night will follow one another.

But not all planets rotate at the same speed. Some rotate faster than the Earth, and others more slowly.

For example, the planet Venus rotates on itself in 243 Earth days. This means that one day on Venus is very very long, and that it is equal to the duration of 243 days on Earth.

GALAXIES

GALAXIES

A galaxy is a huge collection of stars and planets, gas and particles.

There are different shapes of galaxies:

Spiral galaxies are shaped like a flat disk with "tentacles". This gives them a helix shape. This is the most common form of galaxy in the universe.

Elliptical galaxies have an oval shape, more or less stretched. The largest galaxies observed to date are elliptical galaxies. They generally contain many old stars and little interstellar matter (ie gas and dust).

Lenticular galaxies have the shape of a flattened sphere, like a lens. They also have little interstellar matter.

Irregular galaxies do not have a precise shape. Unlike elliptical and lenticular galaxies, they contain a lot of interstellar matter.

Galaxies contain hundreds of billions of stars, and probably as many planets.

Galaxies are not all the same size. There are some gigantic ones, others of medium size, and some smaller ones. Dwarf galaxies (the smallest galaxies) generally contain less than a billion stars.

All galaxies rotate around a central axis called the "galactic center" or "bulge". This area, usually very bright, is composed of stars very close to each other, very dense matter and metals. In most galaxies, this bulge also contains a "supermassive black hole" (we will talk about this later).

Sometimes, some galaxies are approaching each other and collide. Moreover, some spiral galaxies would be the result of a collision and then a merger between two galaxies.

Astronomers still wonder about the birth of galaxies. The most likely hypothesis is that galaxies were originally huge (really huge!) clouds of gas (hydrogen and helium). It is in these clouds that the first stars were formed. Gravitation maintained a certain balance between all this matter, which thus became a galaxy.

However, the gravitation generated by the matter in a galaxy does not seem to be enough to form such a structure.

This is why most astronomers believe that galaxies are filled and surrounded by an invisible matter called dark matter.

DARK MATTER

Dark matter is a hypothetical matter, meaning that we do not really know if it exists or not. Moreover, if it exists, it is not dark, but rather transparent.

This hypothesis was formulated in 1933 by the Swiss astronomer Fritz Zwicky. While studying galaxies and the stars that compose them, he realized that their mass was not sufficient to generate their rotation. Fritz Zwicky then thought that there was an invisible matter (and therefore an invisible mass), but the scientific community of the time rejected this hypothesis.

In the 1970s, this hypothesis was taken up by astronomers, notably by Vera Rubin, an American astronomer who studied the rotational speeds of stars. The term "dark matter" was invented at that time.

Nowadays, astronomers consider that the amount of dark matter is five times greater than the amount of "ordinary" matter in the Universe.

However, no one has ever observed dark matter, and no one knows what it is composed of (if it exists). Its presence is based only on mathematical calculations and suppositions.

The majority of astronomers believe that this dark matter appeared during the Big Bang. This hypothesis can explain many phenomena related to the creation of the Universe.

BLACK HOLES

A black hole is a celestial object whose gravitational force is so strong that nothing can escape, not even light.

A black hole is formed when a very large star dies: When a very large star has burned all its gas (mainly hydrogen and helium), it stops shining. It then collapses on itself (a bit like a house of cards) and, most of the time, explodes into a Supernova. This explosion does not usually destroy the whole star. Sometimes, its remaining mass becomes so dense that its gravitational force compresses it into a black hole. This is called a stellar black hole.
A black hole is not really a hole. It is a rather small but very dense object. It is as if a tennis ball had the mass of 500 elephants. A very large gravitational force is therefore concentrated in a small object. Now imagine that this small ball is a magnet. It would have a considerable force of attraction while remaining tiny.

Supermassive black holes are formed in the same way, but in larger proportions. And as we have seen, almost all galaxies have a supermassive black hole at their center. This black hole, due to its very strong gravitational force, drives the rotation of the galaxy. Everything that passes too close to a black hole is therefore subject to an extreme gravitational force, and is therefore "swallowed".

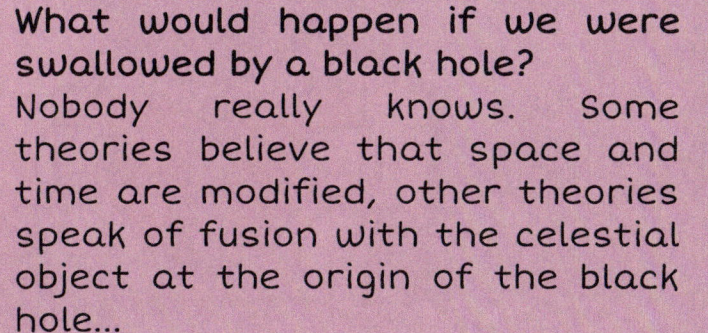

What would happen if we were swallowed by a black hole?
Nobody really knows. Some theories believe that space and time are modified, other theories speak of fusion with the celestial object at the origin of the black hole...

THE MILKY WAY

The galaxy in which our planet is located is called the Milky Way.

It is a spiral galaxy. It is a tiny part of an arm of this spiral that can be seen in the sky, in the form of a white band.

The Milky Way is an old galaxy, since it was formed between 10 and 12 billion years ago.
It is composed of about 200 billion stars according to NASA (American space agency). One of these stars is our Sun!

It is also a very large galaxy: Traveling at the speed of light, it would take about 100 000 years to cross it.

At the center of our galaxy is a huge supermassive black hole, named "Sagittarius A*". The mass of this black hole is equivalent to 4 million times that of our sun.

The closest galaxy to ours is the Andromeda galaxy. Moreover, scientists estimate that these two galaxies will collide in about 3 billion years.

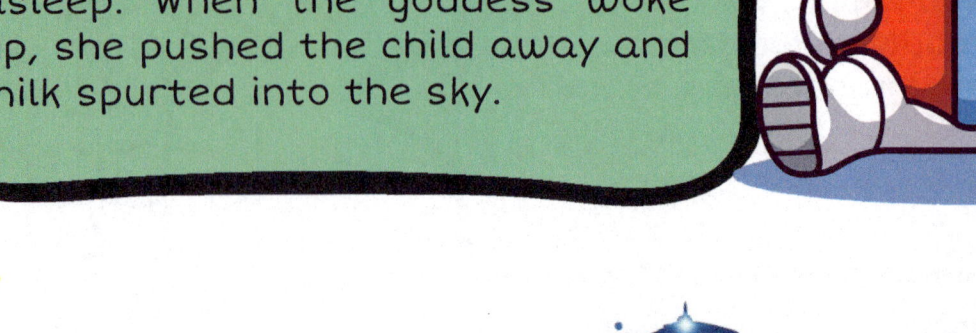

The name of our galaxy comes from Greek mythology: According to the legend, Heracles (son of Zeus), who was still a young child, would have sucked the breast of the goddess Hera, who had fallen asleep. When the goddess woke up, she pushed the child away and milk spurted into the sky.

Photograph of a portion of the Milky Way.
Photo credit: JCOMP / Freepik.com

SOLAR SYSTEM

THE SOLAR SYSTEM

Our planetary system is called the solar system. It is composed of the Sun (which is a star), 8 planets (Mercury, Venus, Earth, Mars, Jupiter, Saturn, Uranus, and Neptune), their satellites, and various celestial objects (asteroids, comets ...).

The solar system was born 4.5 billion years ago and is therefore part of the Milky Way.

At the beginning, it was only a huge cloud of matter, probably resulting from the explosion of a Supernova.

Between Mars and Jupiter is an asteroid belt. Moreover, our solar system was subjected to large bombardments of asteroids about 4 billion years ago.

All the planets of the solar system revolve around the Sun, at a different speed from each other. Moreover, each planet is positioned at a different distance from the sun (if this were not the case, they would collide while rotating!).

It is this phenomenon of revolution that defines the length of a year: For example, the Earth goes around the Sun in 365 days (a Earth year lasts 365 days). Saturn, which is further from the Sun than the Earth, goes around the Sun in 10 759 Earth days. A year on Saturn lasts 10759 Earth days.

As we have already seen, each planet rotates on itself, and again at a different speed from each other. The rotation defines the length of a day (day + night) of a planet. The Earth makes a complete turn on itself in 24 hours (the duration of a Earth day is therefore 24 hours). On Saturn, a day lasts only 10:30 hours.

All the planets of our solar system have a name of a god or goddess of the Roman mythology, except the Earth.

1 Mercury
2 Venus
3 Earth
4 Mars
5 Jupiter
6 Saturn
7 Uranus
8 Neptune

THE SUN

Name : Sun

Type : Yellow dwarf star

Rotation time : 27 Earth days

Average surface temperature : 5500 °C / 9900 °F

Diameter : 1.4 million km / 870 000 Miles

Distance from the Earth : 149,6 million km / 93 million Miles

The Sun is the star of our solar system.

Astronomers classify our sun as a yellow dwarf. Like most stars, it is composed of hydrogen and helium.

The sun is the largest celestial object in our solar system: it represents 99.85% of the total mass of our planetary system.

The temperature of its surface is 5500 degrees Celsius (9900 degrees Fahrenheit). It is therefore impossible to approach the sun without being totally burned.

The temperature of its center (in the middle of the sun) is even hotter! About 15 million degrees Celsius (27 million degrees Fahrenheit).

Sometimes the temperature of its surface drops in places and causes spots, which can be observed with a telescope or an adapted telescope.

The sun transmits to the planets of our system a quantity of energy called solar radiation. This radiation is in more or less quantity according to the distance between the sun and the planets.

On Earth, this solar radiation brings us light and heat. These elements are of primary importance in the appearance of life on our planet.

The solar radiation also influences the climate and weather phenomena.

One day, our sun will disappear, like all the stars. Astronomers estimate that this event will occur in about 5 billion years.
Under the effect of pressure, the sun will first of all grow enormously. It will become 200 times larger! The nearby planets will be pulverized. Then, it will shrink very quickly. All its matter will escape into space, except for its core, which will cool down and become a white dwarf the size of the Earth.

MERCURY

Name : Mercury

Type : Telluric planet

Rotation time : 58 Earth days

Revolution time : 88 Earth days

Average surface temperature : between 400 and -150 °C / between 750 and -240 °F

Diameter : 4800 Km / 3000 Miles

Distance from the Earth : 92 million km / 57 million Miles

Mercury is the closest planet to the sun (58 million km / 36 million Miles). It is also the smallest planet in our solar system (about 3 times smaller than the Earth).

Mercury is a telluric planet and its core is mainly composed of metals. There is no satellite around the planet.

On Mercury, temperatures are extreme: During the day (i.e. on the part exposed to the sun), the temperature is 400 degrees Celsius (750 degrees Fahrenheit). At night (so on the part not exposed to the sun), it is -150 degrees Celsius (-240 degrees Fahrenheit). This temperature difference is explained by the absence of atmosphere around Mercury. The surface of the planet is very hot during the day because it is very close to the sun. But at night, since there is no atmosphere to retain heat, it cools down very quickly.

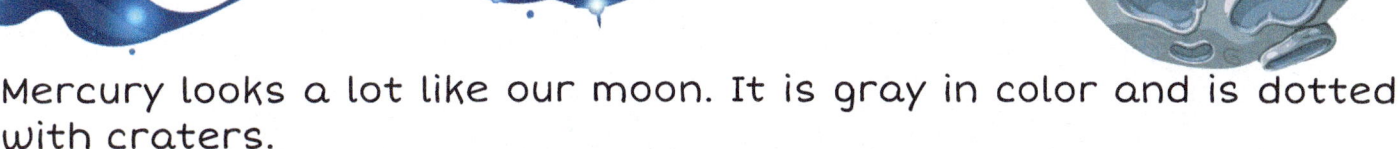

Mercury looks a lot like our moon. It is gray in color and is dotted with craters.

Mercury is the fastest planet in the solar system. It revolves around the Sun at a speed of 172 000 Km/h (107 000 mph). It takes 88 Earth days to go around the Sun.

On the other hand, its speed of rotation is slow. It turns on itself in 58 days.

This means that on Mercury, one year (revolution around the Sun) lasts one day and a half (rotation of the planet on itself)!

VENUS

Name : Venus

Type : Telluric planet

Rotation time : 243 Earth days

Revolution time : 224 Earth days

Average surface temperature : 450 °C / 840 ° F

Diameter : 12104 Km / 7521 Miles

Distance from the Earth : 41 million km / 25 million Miles

The planet Venus is the brightest object in our sky, after the sun and the moon. However, Venus is a planet, not a star. It does not produce light but reflects that of the sun.

Venus is sometimes called "the star shepherd". Generally, it appears in the sky at sunset and just before dawn. It was the first planet to be observed, and some documents about it date back to 2000 years BC.

On Venus, it is very hot (about 450 degrees Celsius / 840 degrees Fahrenheit). This heat comes from its proximity to the sun, but not only.

Venus has a very dense atmosphere, mainly composed of carbon dioxide. The atmospheric pressure is 90 times higher than on Earth. If a human lands on Venus, he will be crushed by the weight of the air. This dense atmosphere causes a very important greenhouse effect (which retains heat).

Venus is sometimes considered as the twin sister of the Earth. Like the Earth, Venus is a telluric planet, and they are almost identical in size. On Venus, there are also mountains, volcanoes, plains... There are even clouds (but on Venus, they are composed of sulfur dioxide and sulfuric acid!). Finally, Venus is the closest planet to the Earth.

But unlike the Earth, Venus has no satellite. Moreover, it turns upside down: Its direction of rotation is reversed compared to the other planets of the solar system.

Astronomers think that this inverted rotation could have been caused by a very powerful collision with another celestial object during its formation phase.

Venus has another peculiarity: A day on Venus lasts longer than a year! Venus turns around the sun in 224 Earth days and turns on itself in 243 Earth days. Its duration of rotation is thus greater than its duration of revolution. If we lived on Venus, a year would be shorter than a day.

EARTH

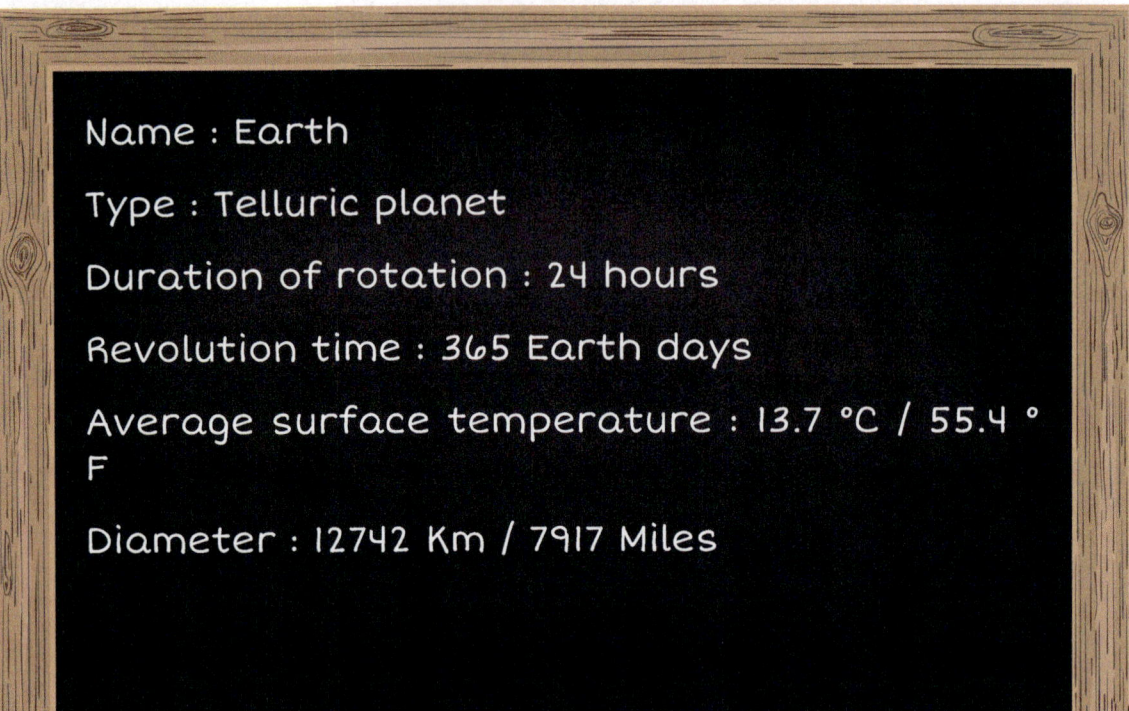

Name : Earth

Type : Telluric planet

Duration of rotation : 24 hours

Revolution time : 365 Earth days

Average surface temperature : 13.7 °C / 55.4 °F

Diameter : 12742 Km / 7917 Miles

Earth is the planet where we live.

It is the 3rd closest planet to the sun (after Mercury and Venus). The distance between the Earth and the Sun is 149 597 800 km (92 955 700 Miles).
It is also the fifth largest planet in the solar system, and it has only one satellite (the moon).

When the Earth was born, its surface was molten, made of rocks so hot that they were liquid (like lava). Then the Earth cooled and a crust formed on its surface.

Generally speaking, the Earth is composed of iron (30%), oxygen (30%), silicon (15%), magnesium (14%), then calcium, aluminum, carbon...

The Earth's atmosphere, whose average thickness is 600 km (372 Miles), is mainly composed of nitrogen and oxygen.

The Earth is the densest planet in the solar system, i.e. it contains the most matter in relation to its size.
70% of its surface is covered with water (mostly liquid, but also solid). The remaining 30% is made of rocks (continents, islands...).

But where does this water come from?
We don't really know. We must already know that water is a molecule composed of two hydrogen atoms and one oxygen atom. These elements are very present on our planet. This water was probably "manufactured" at the time of the creation of the Earth, first in the form of vapor (thus of clouds), then in liquid form by condensation (and thus of rain).
But the large quantity of water present on Earth could also have been partially brought by comets and asteroids that came to crash on our planet. Indeed, comets and asteroids are partly formed of ice (i.e. solid water).

The Earth's core is composed of 2 parts: The inner core is composed mainly of iron (80%) and nickel. Its thickness is about 1200 km (745 Miles). This inner core is solid.

The outer core, also mostly composed of iron, is liquid (i.e. the material is in fusion). Its thickness is 2200 km (1360 Miles).

The temperature of the core varies between 3800 and 5500 degrees Celsius (6870 and 9900 degrees Fahrenheit) depending on the depth.

The Earth's mantle surrounds the core. It has an average thickness of 2880 km (1790 Miles) and is mostly composed of rocks. The mantle is also divided into 2 parts: The upper mantle, close to the crust, and the lower mantle, close to the core.

Its temperature is about 2000 degrees Celsius (3600 degrees Fahrenheit) for the upper part and 3500 degrees Celsius (6300 degrees Fahrenheit) for the lower part.

We often imagine that the mantle is composed of molten and liquid rocks, like the lava of a volcano. This is not true. The mantle is made of very hot rocks, but it is solid. But inside this mantle, the matter moves (very very slowly). Sometimes this movement causes a large heat spot just below the crust. At this point, the rock melts and becomes effectively liquid. Sometimes, the pressure causes this rock to rise and form a volcano.

These movements of the mantle impact the earth's crust, which in turn moves and causes different phenomena, such as the movement of continents, the formation of mountains, or earthquakes.

The Earth's crust is the surface of the Earth. It is composed of rocks (continents and islands), but also of water (seas and oceans). Its average thickness is about 30 km (18.5 Miles).

1 Inner core
2 Outer core
3 Lower mantle
4 Upper mantle
5 Earth's crust

67

THE MOON

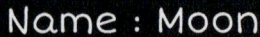

Name : Moon

Type : Satellite

Rotation time : 27 Earth days

Revolution time (around the Earth) : 27 Earth days

Average surface temperature : between 120 and -250 °C / between 250 and -480 °F

Diameter : 3474 Km / 2158 Miles

Distance from the Earth : 384 400 km / 239 000 Miles

The moon is the only satellite of the Earth. It formed about 60 million years after our solar system. Astronomers believe that a planet in formation collided with the Earth (itself in formation). The shock tore a large amount of material from the two celestial objects, and this material was thrown into orbit around the Earth. This debris then stuck to each other, under the effect of gravitation, to form the moon.

The moon is essentially composed of silicon, aluminum, iron, calcium, and magnesium. Its atmosphere is almost non-existent.

The surface of the moon is covered with craters. We can even see some of them from Earth. These craters were made by comet and asteroid impacts. On the visible side of the moon, there are at least 300,000 craters over one kilometer (0.62 Miles) in diameter.

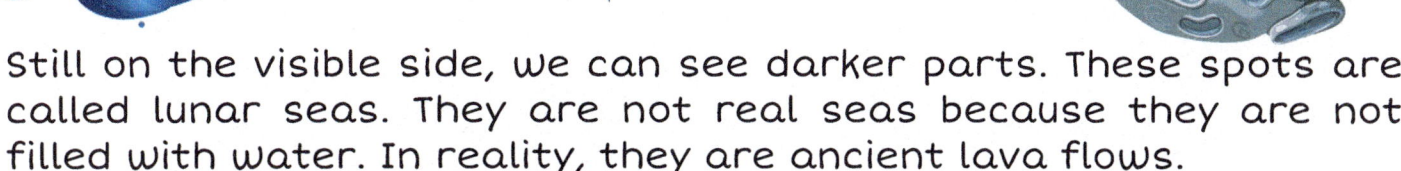

Still on the visible side, we can see darker parts. These spots are called lunar seas. They are not real seas because they are not filled with water. In reality, they are ancient lava flows.

The rotation and revolution (around the Earth) of the moon have the same duration (27 days). This explains why we always see the same side of the moon.

If we walk on the moon, we float (well almost). The moon is smaller than the Earth, and its gravitational force is 6 times less. So, on the moon, we weigh 6 times less than on Earth. If we jump, we fall back 6 times slower, hence this impression of floating.

On the moon, the temperature can rise to more than 120°C (250°F) during the day, but also drop to -250°C (-480°F) at night.

Seen from the Earth, the moon is sometimes round, sometimes in the shape of a crescent, or a semicircle. This depends on its position relative to the sun. When the moon is between the Earth and the Sun, we do not see it anymore, because its visible side from the Earth is in shadow. When it is out of alignment with the Earth-Sun, we see it in the shape of a crescent or semicircle, because its visible side is partially illuminated by the Sun. Finally, when the moon is on the other side of the Earth (from the sun), it is the full moon because its visible side is fully lit.

MARS

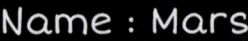

Name : Mars

Type : Telluric planet

Rotation time : 24 hours and 30 minutes

Revolution time : 687 Earth days

Average surface temperature : -63 °C / -81 °F

Diameter : 6779 Km / 4212 Miles

Distance from the Earth : 78 million km / 48.5 million Miles

Mars is the fourth telluric planet of the solar system.

Its surface is composed of craters, volcanoes, plains, dunes and crevasses. Moreover, the highest volcano in the solar system is located on the planet Mars and is called Olympus Mons.

Mars is also often called the red planet. Indeed, in the sky, it has red and orange glows. This color comes from its soil, which contains iron oxide (i.e. rusty iron).

The atmosphere of Mars is thin and is mainly composed of carbon dioxide.

Mars has 2 satellites, Phobos and Deimos. These satellites are not really spherical and are rather asteroid shaped.
They are also small in size. Phobos measures 27 km (16.7 Miles) and Deimos 15 km (9.3 Miles).

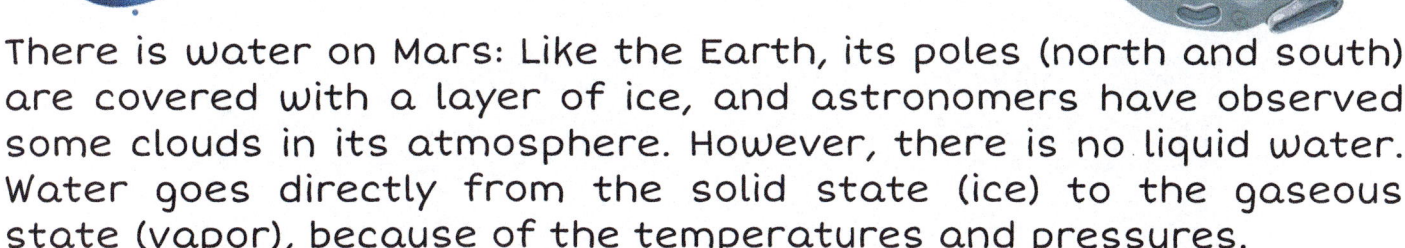

There is water on Mars: Like the Earth, its poles (north and south) are covered with a layer of ice, and astronomers have observed some clouds in its atmosphere. However, there is no liquid water. Water goes directly from the solid state (ice) to the gaseous state (vapor), because of the temperatures and pressures.

However, a very long time ago, when Mars was a very young planet, there was liquid water. Astronomers have even discovered dry rivers.

Since the 1960s, we have been sending space probes to Mars. We have even sent robots since the 2000s to study the red planet.

The planet Mars has greatly influenced science fiction. In fact, in books and movies, Martians are the inhabitants of Mars!

JUPITER

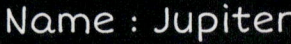

Name : Jupiter

Type : Gaseous planet

Rotation time : 9 hours and 55 minutes

Revolution time : 4333 Earth days

Average surface temperature : -160 °C / -250 °F

Diameter : 143 000 Km / 88 850 Miles

Distance from the Earth : 628 million km / 390 million Miles

Jupiter is the closest gas planet to the sun, and the largest planet in the solar system. Its mass is greater than that of all the other planets combined.

The composition of Jupiter is close to that of the Sun. It has a solid core but all the rest of the planet is composed of gas (mainly hydrogen and helium). Its surface is therefore not solid and it is impossible to "walk on Jupiter".

The atmosphere of Jupiter is composed of huge cloudy bands of different colors (white, brown, brown). This difference in color is mainly due to the altitude of these clouds and their composition.

These gaseous bands are swept by violent winds, up to 600 km/h (372 mph).

A large red spot is also visible on the surface of Jupiter. It is in fact a giant anticyclone, the size of the Earth.

Jupiter is easily observable from Earth. It is the 4th brightest celestial object in our sky (behind the sun, the moon, and Venus).

Jupiter is the planet of the solar system which has the fastest rotation: It makes a turn on itself in less than 10 hours. On the other hand, it takes almost 12 Earth years to go around the Sun.

There are 79 satellites around Jupiter. The first were discovered by Galileo in 1610.
Jupiter has the largest satellite in the solar system. This satellite, called "Ganymede" is larger than the planet Mercury.

Finally, Jupiter is also surrounded by very thin rings, composed of dust and small debris of meteoric origin. These rings are very difficult to observe from Earth, given their thinness.

SATURN

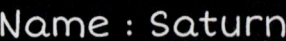

Name : Saturn

Type : Gaseous planet

Rotation time : 10 hours and 30 minutes

Revolution time : 10 759 Earth days

Average surface temperature : -180 °C / -290 °F

Diameter : 116 460 Km / 72 364 Miles

Distance from the Earth : 1.3 billion km / 808 million Miles

Saturn is the second largest planet in the solar system, behind Jupiter.

This gaseous planet is made of hydrogen at more than 95%, and helium, and has a core most certainly made of rock and iron.
Its atmosphere is swept by very powerful winds, up to 1800 km/h (1120 mph).

Saturn is a relatively cold planet (-180°C / -290°F). It makes a complete rotation in only 10 hours and 30 minutes. It takes Saturn a little more than 29 Earth years to make a complete revolution around the Sun.

Saturn has the particularity to be surrounded by a very large ring system, whose diameter is about 360 000 km (224 000 Miles).

These rings are composed of more than 95% ice. They are so large that it is possible to observe them from Earth with a pair of binoculars.

Saturn is the planet with the largest number of satellites (82 in total). There are also hundreds of objects (asteroids for example) orbiting the planet.

Its largest satellite is a moon called Titan. It is the 2nd largest satellite in the solar system, behind Ganymede (satellite of Jupiter).

Titan is formed of rocks and ice, and has a dense atmosphere and lakes of hydrocarbons (oil and gas). Scientists believe that Titan could possibly host microbial life (alien microbes!).

URANUS

Name : Uranus

Type : Gaseous planet

Rotation time : 17 hours and 14 minutes

Revolution time : 30 685 Earth days

Average surface temperature : -220 °C / -364 °F

Diameter : 50 724 Km / 31518 Miles

Distance from the Earth : 2.3 billion km / 1.43 billion Miles

Uranus is a gas planet (ice giant type), and the 3rd largest planet of our solar system. It is also the coldest planet.

Its atmosphere is mainly composed of hydrogen and helium. Its core is composed of rocks, iron and nickel. Around its core is the mantle, made of ice, methane and ammonia. It is the methane (which is a gas) that gives Uranus its blue color.

Uranus has 27 satellites, and 13 rings.

A day on Uranus is equal to 17 hours and 14 minutes. Its revolution around the Sun is 84 Earth years.

Like Venus, Uranus has a reversed direction of rotation. Moreover, the rotation axis of Uranus is almost perpendicular to the rotation axes of the other planets.

If we could observe the whole solar system, we would have the impression that the planets turn on themselves like spinning tops, except Uranus, which would roll like a marble on a table. This is why Uranus is sometimes called the lying planet.

Uranus was discovered late. To be exact, Uranus is visible in the sky, but everyone thought it was a star. John Flamsteed, an English astronomer, named it "34 Tauri". This name comes from the fact that Uranus was observable at that time in the constellation of Taurus.

It was in 1781 that William Herschel, a German musician, discovered that this star was not a star. William Herschel was an amateur astronomer but could not afford to buy a telescope. He therefore made one himself.
While searching for stars from the garden of his house, he discovered Uranus.

At first, he thought it was a comet and told the scientific community about his discovery. In 1783, Uranus was officially recognized as a planet.

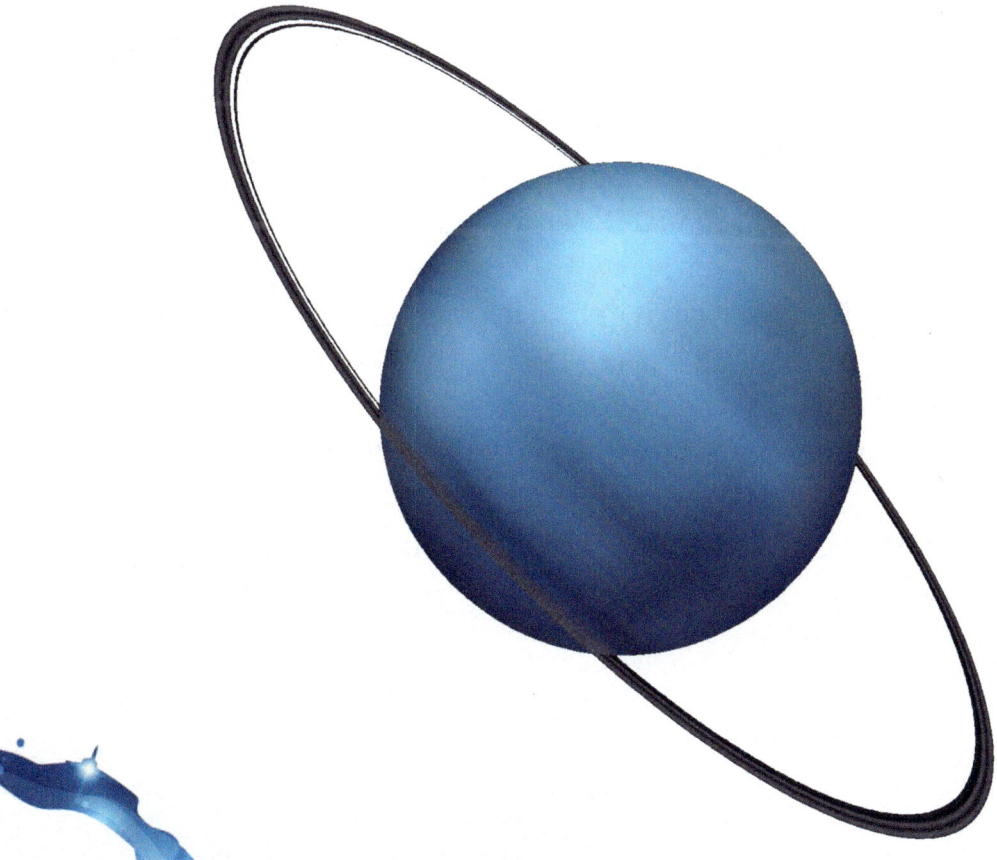

NEPTUNE

Name : Neptune

Type : Gaseous planet

Duration of rotation : 16 hours

Revolution time : 60 266 Earth days

Average surface temperature : between -200 °C / -328 °F

Diameter : 49 244 Km / 30 599 Miles

Distance from the Earth : 4.3 billion km / 2.7 billion Miles

Neptune is the last planet of the solar system.

Neptune is a giant ice planet. Its composition is almost the same as Uranus, and its blue color is also due to the presence of methane.

Neptune is also the planet that takes the longest time to go around the Sun, in more than 60 000 days (about 165 Earth years).

Because it is so far from our planet, Neptune could not be well observed before 1846, because we did not have a telescope powerful enough. However, astronomers knew that this planet existed. Its discovery was made thanks to mathematics!

Like Uranus, astronomers thought that Neptune was simply a distant star.

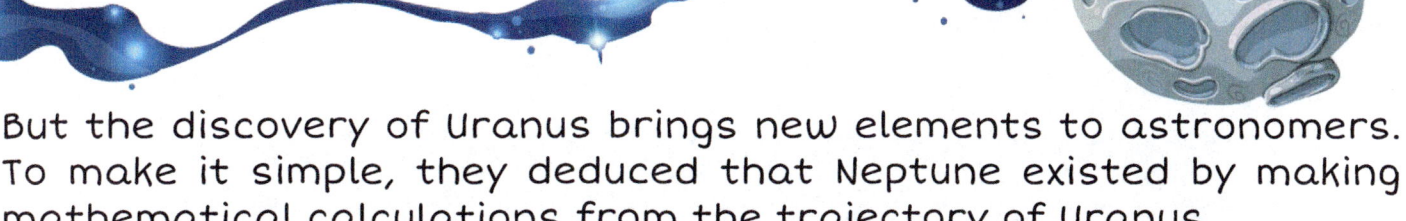

But the discovery of Uranus brings new elements to astronomers. To make it simple, they deduced that Neptune existed by making mathematical calculations from the trajectory of Uranus.

It is on Neptune that we find the most violent winds of the solar system. They can reach 2100 km/h (1300 mph).

Neptune has 14 satellites.

The largest of them is called Triton. This satellite has the particularity to turn in the opposite direction of Neptune. Astronomers believe that Triton could be an ancient dwarf planet captured by the gravitational force of Neptune.

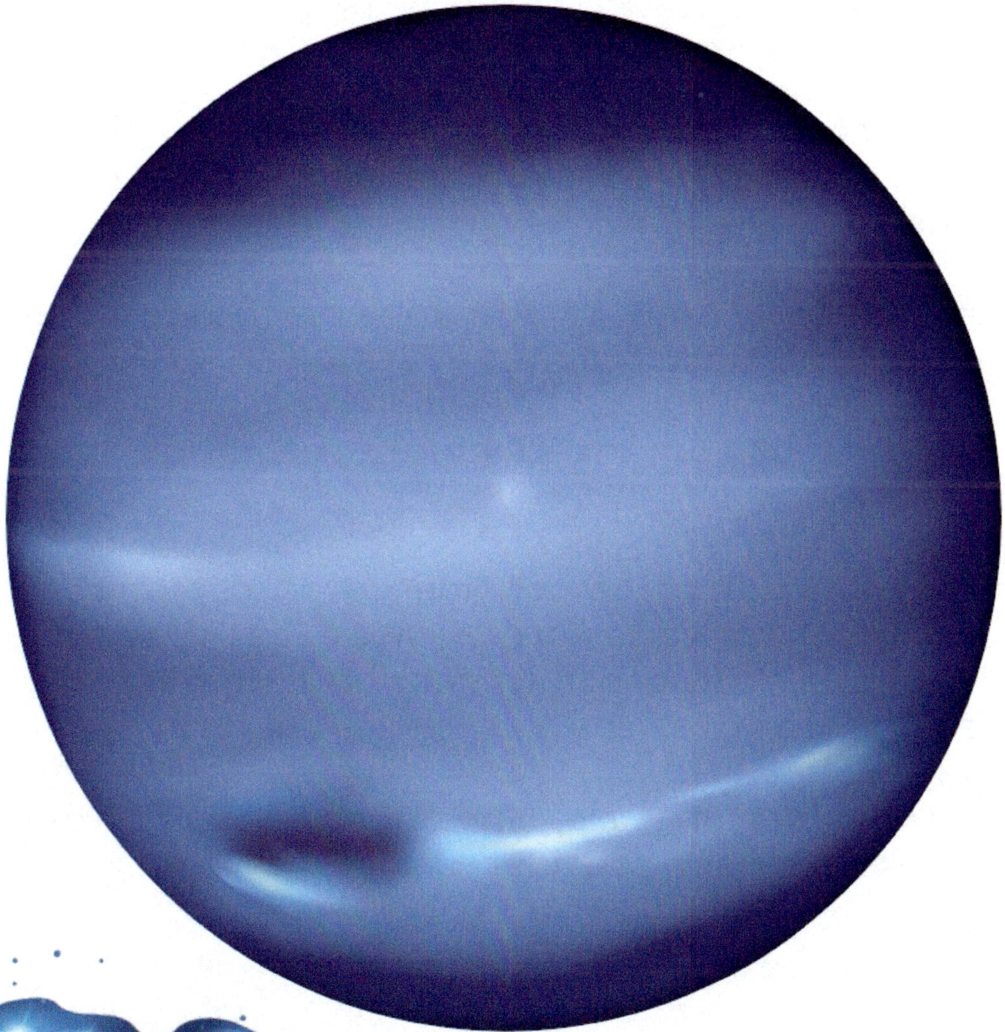

PLUTO

Name : Pluto

Type : Dwarf planet

Rotation time : 6 Earth days, 9 hours and 17 minutes

Revolution time : 90 588 Earth days

Average surface temperature : -220 °C / -364 F

Diameter : 2377 Km / 1477 Miles

Distance from the Earth : between 4.5 and 7.3 billion km / between 2.7 and 4.5 billion Miles

Pluto is a dwarf planet, smaller than our moon, and discovered in 1930. At that time, astronomers considered Pluto to be the 9th planet in the solar system.

Since then, our knowledge of the universe has evolved, and Pluto was classified as a dwarf planet in 2006.

A dwarf planet is an intermediate celestial object between asteroids and planets.

For a celestial object to be considered as a planet, its orbit (i.e. its trajectory around its star) must be free of any object (asteroids, debris...). In other words, nothing must be in the path of a planet and its satellites.

This is not the case for Pluto, whose orbit is full of asteroids. This is why Pluto is no longer considered a planet.

Pluto is composed of rocks, frozen water, and frozen gas (methane and nitrogen).

Pluto has 5 satellites. This set is called the Plutonian system.

The largest satellite of Pluto is called Charon, and has a diameter of 1207 km (750 Miles). Given their small difference in mass, the two celestial objects attract each other. Thus, Charon revolves around Pluto, and Pluto rotates around an eccentric axis of rotation, unlike the other planets. If we could observe them, we would have the impression that they are dancing a waltz together.

Pluto orbits the Sun in over 164 Earth years. Its orbit around the Sun is not circular but elliptical, which makes the dwarf planet move away from and towards the Sun during its revolution.

Finally, the orbit of Pluto is not on the same plane as the 8 planets of the solar system. While the planets turn "flat", Pluto has an orbit inclined by 17°.

ECLIPSES

An eclipse is the momentary disappearance (total or partial) of a celestial object in the shadow of another celestial object.

On Earth, there are 2 kinds of eclipses:

Solar eclipses: When the moon is placed between the sun and the Earth, it prevents the light of the sun from reaching our planet (or more exactly a part of our planet).

Lunar eclipses: When the Earth is placed between the sun and the moon, it prevents the sunlight from reaching our satellite.

The most spectacular eclipses are total solar eclipses. They occur when the moon completely hides the sun. In this case, the moon casts its shadow on the Earth, and suddenly, the day darkens as if it were night.

An eclipse usually lasts only a few minutes.

Be careful, to observe an eclipse, you must always have protective glasses, because when the sun reappears, its rays are dangerous for our eyes.

Illustration of a solar eclipse seen from the Earth.

THE 4 SEASONS

On Earth, there are 4 seasons: Spring, Summer, Fall, and Winter.

The main phenomenon explaining the seasons is the rotation of the Earth.

The Earth turns on itself around an axis, and this axis is tilted by 23.5°. The inclination of this axis makes that, depending on the time of the year, the parts of our planet most exposed to the sun's rays are not always the same.

For example, in July, the northern hemisphere is more exposed to the sun's rays than the southern hemisphere. It is therefore summer in the Northern Hemisphere and winter in the Southern Hemisphere.

But in January, it is the opposite. The Earth has made a half turn around the sun. The southern hemisphere receives more rays than the northern hemisphere. It is therefore summer in the southern hemisphere and winter in the northern hemisphere.

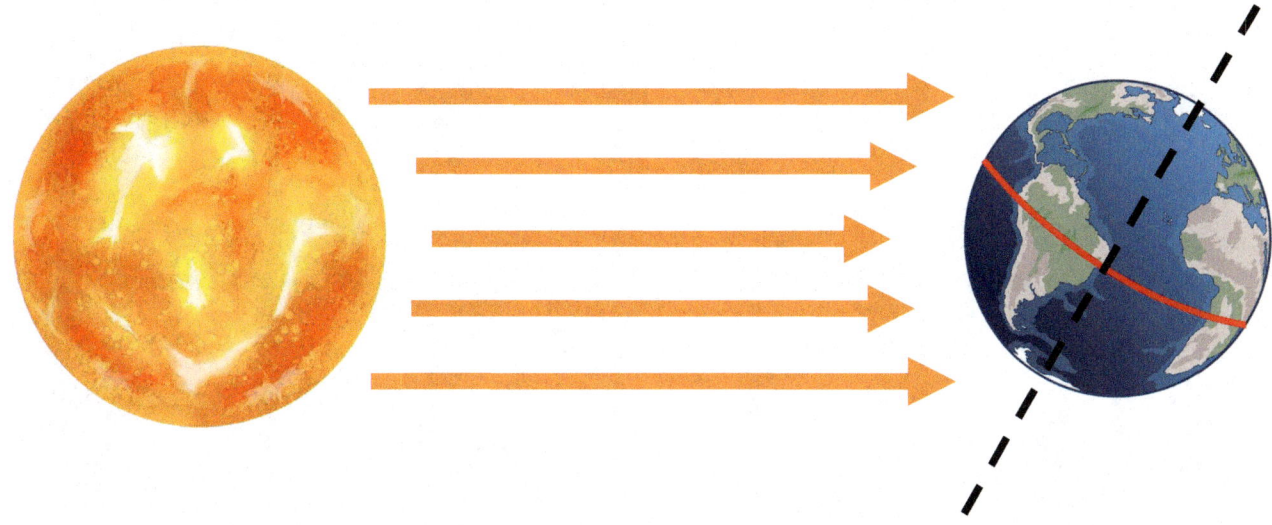

As for spring and autumn, they are intermediate seasons. They are a kind of transitional season between summer and winter.

On the other planets too there can be seasons, or not!

For example, on Venus, there is no season. Its axis of rotation is very little inclined, and its very thick atmosphere retains a lot of heat. So, on Venus, it is always summer (with a temperature of 450°C / 840°F).

On Mars, which is very similar to Earth, there are seasons. However, even in summer it is very cold. And since Mars has no vegetation, no trees bloom in spring!

There are only two seasons on Uranus: summer and winter. The tilt of the planet being very pronounced, each season lasts 42 years. And when one hemisphere receives the sun's rays, the other one remains in the shadow (during 42 years).

HUMANS IN SPACE

SPACE EXPLORATION

Humans have been observing the sky for thousands of years, but space exploration is very recent.

Space exploration is the physical exploration of anything outside our planet. To physically explore a celestial object, it is necessary to send men or machines.

We had to wait for the technological advances of the middle of the 20th century to consider going into space.

However, long before that, writers had imagined space travel.

For example, in the 2nd century, the Greek philosopher Lucian of Samosate published a story in which a sailing ship finds itself in space because of a storm.

In the 19th century, Jules Vernes, a French writer, fascinated his readers with two novels about lunar exploration.

The novel entitled "From the Earth to the Moon" was published in 1865. The story takes place at the end of the American Civil War. A group of American artillerymen and a French adventurer join forces and create a cannon capable of sending them to the moon. The novel "Around the Moon", a sequel to the first book, was published 4 years later.

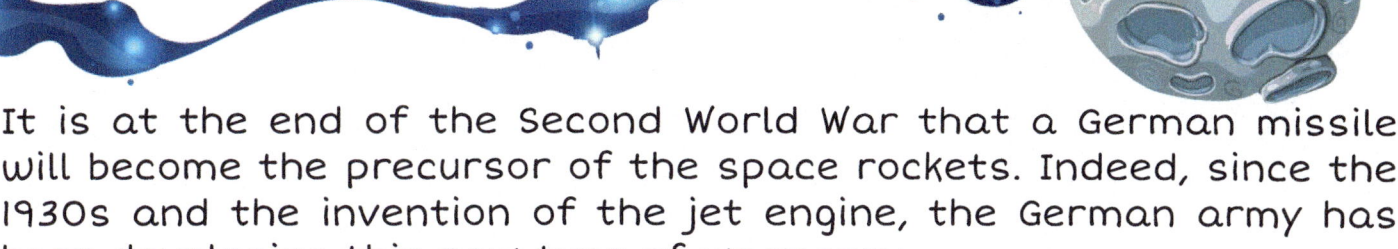

It is at the end of the Second World War that a German missile will become the precursor of the space rockets. Indeed, since the 1930s and the invention of the jet engine, the German army has been developing this new type of weaponry.

In 1944, a German missile called V2 was the first object to reach an altitude of 100 km (62 Miles). This type of missile was widely used to bomb London (England) and Antwerp (Belgium).

When the war ended, the United States of America and the USSR were very interested in the V2 and analyzed this new technology thanks to the material recovered in Germany. The two countries will also recruit the principal German engineers having worked on the V2.

England proceeded with V2 launch experiments with the help of the United States. On its side, France recruits about thirty German specialists to work on a project of development of rocket.

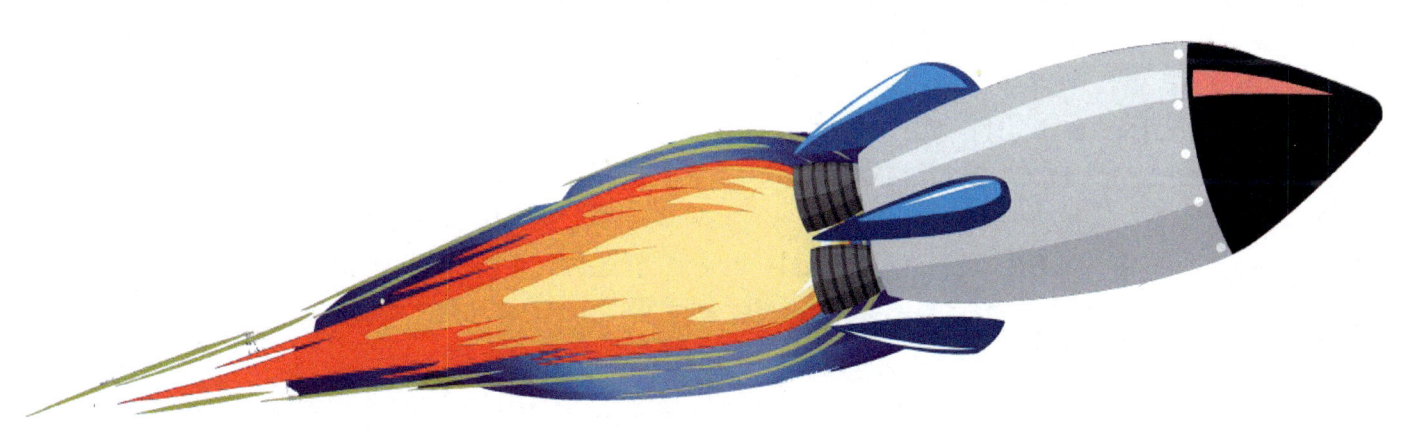

SPUTNIK 1

Sputnik I is the name of the very first artificial satellite launched into orbit around the Earth.

After the Second World War and based on the technology of the German V2, Russia (which at that time was called the USSR or Soviet Union) developed a missile capable of carrying an atomic bomb over a great distance.

Sergei Korolev is the person in charge of this project. An engineer of Ukrainian origin, he was also passionate about astronomy.

In 1957, this new missile made its first test flight. Sergueï then persuaded the Soviet authorities to use this missile to send a satellite in orbit around the Earth.

Sergei Korolev built a small satellite capable of recording certain data in space (temperatures, concentration of electrons...). This satellite, named Sputnik I, is an aluminum sphere of 58 centimeters in diameter (22.8") equipped with 4 antennas.

On October 4, 1957, Sputnik I is launched from a base located in Kazakhstan. About 5 minutes later, it entered into orbit around the Earth.

Sputnik I remains in orbit for a little more than 3 months, but loses more and more altitude.

On January 4, 1958, the satellite enters the Earth's atmosphere and is destroyed. Sputnik I made 1400 times the turn of the Earth.

EXPLORER 1

Explorer 1 was the first American satellite to orbit the Earth.

When Sputnik 1 was launched, the United States did not intend to let the USSR take the lead in the conquest of space.

In less than 3 months, American engineers will develop a launcher (i.e. a rocket) and a satellite.

Explorer 1 is a small satellite, very elongated (like a small rocket), measuring 2 meters (80") and weighing only 14 kilograms (31 pounds).

It was launched on February 1, 1958 from Cape Canaveral, Florida.

Equipped with a cosmic ray detector, Explorer 1 will allow many discoveries, including the "Van Allen Belt", which is a concentration of energy particles.

The satellite stopped transmitting 111 days later because its batteries were exhausted. But it remains in orbit around the Earth for 12 years. On March 31, 1970, it enters our atmosphere and is destroyed.

THE OTHER SATELLITES

Since the launches of Sputnik 1 and Explorer 1, many other satellites have been launched, by many different countries.

Currently, there are more than 2000 satellites around the Earth.

Not all satellites have the same purpose. There are communication satellites, observation satellites, military satellites...

The majority of satellites orbit the Earth in low orbit, i.e. at an altitude of less than 1000 kilometers (620 Miles). These satellites are mainly used for meteorological observations, earth observation and certain types of communication (military for example).

The satellites in medium orbit, between 1000 and 30 000 kilometers of altitude (between 620 and 18 640 Miles), are used for location (GPS for example), and some military communications.

The satellites in high orbit, at more than 35 000 kilometers of altitude (21 750 Miles), are mainly communication satellites (television, radio, telephone) and space observation. These satellites are geostationary, which means that they are always above the same point on the Earth.

Satellites should not be confused with space probes. Satellites are in orbit around the Earth, while probes are sent into space, well beyond the Earth's orbit. Some probes are also designed to orbit other celestial objects, such as the moon (LRO satellite), the Sun (SOHO satellite), Mars (Mars Odyssey and Mars Express satellites), or Jupiter (Galileo and Juno satellites).

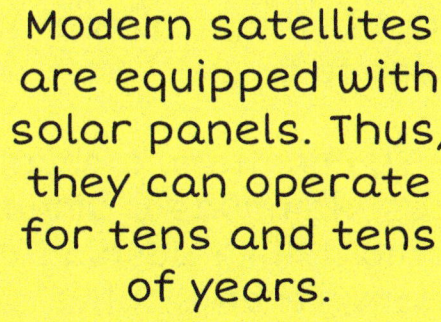

Modern satellites are equipped with solar panels. Thus, they can operate for tens and tens of years.

LAÏKA, HAM, AND THE OTHERS

In order to know if men could survive in space, scientists first conducted tests with animals.

The first test took place in the United States in 1947: flies were sent to an altitude of over 100 km (62 Miles) with a V2.
In 1948, still in the United States, a macaque named Albert was the first mammal sent into space. Unfortunately, he died of suffocation. In 1950, it is the turn of a mouse which dies at its return on Earth, during the landing.

On November 3, 1957, the USSR sends a dog named Laika in space, on board Sputnik 2. Laika is a 3 years old stray dog, found in Moscow.
7 hours after the launch, Laïka dies (probably because of the stress and a too high temperature). Her capsule remains in orbit 5 months then is destroyed while entering the atmosphere.
The Soviet scientists admitted that Laïka could not have survived its voyage. Its capsule could not resist the entry in the atmosphere.

In 1960, the USSR sends several animals at the same time in space. There are two dogs, a rabbit, two rats, forty mice, flies, but also plants. They are the first animals to have returned alive from their space travel.

On January 31, 1961, Ham, a chimpanzee, was sent into space by the United States. Ham was trained and had to perform various tasks during the flight (like pushing a lever for example). The trip goes well and Ham returns alive. After that, he was sent to the Washington Zoo until his death in 1983.

On October 18, 1963, France sends in space a cat named Félicette. Her capsule stayed 9 minutes in space and then returned to Earth. Félicette returned alive.

Many other animals have been sent into space and unfortunately, many of them did not come back alive.

Moreover, in several countries (United States, France, USSR, England...) several animal protection associations have expressed their dissatisfaction about these experiments.

Nowadays, some animals accompany astronauts in space, to conduct experiments (effects of space travel, reproduction...). But they are small animals, like lizards, flies, or blobs.

GAGARINE, SHEPARD, AND THE OTHERS

Yuri Gagarin was the first man to fly in space.

Yuri was born in 1934 in the USSR. In 1941, his country entered the war with Germany. One day, a Soviet plane lands near the village where the Gagarin family lives. This event will mark Youri, who is fascinated by this plane and its pilot.

When the war ended, Yuri went back to school. A few years later, he became an agricultural mechanic. But Yuri wanted to become a pilot. So he took flying lessons in an amateur club, then joined the army, in a military flying school. He then became a fighter pilot.

Three years later, Youri is selected to participate in the Soviet space program. At the beginning, there are 3000 candidates. Youri Gagarin will finally be chosen, for his skills, but also for his size. Youri measures only 1.58 meters (5ft 2in), which is an ideal size considering the little space available in the capsule.

On April 12, 1961, Youri Gagarin takes off towards space. He makes a 2 hours trip in orbit then returns to Earth. His capsule enters the atmosphere then, with a few kilometers with the top of the ground, Gagarin ejects and finishes his descent in parachute. He becomes then a hero for the USSR.

On March 27, 1968, Yuri died in a plane accident during a training flight.

Alan Shepard is the first American to have travelled in space.

Alan was born in 1923 in the United States. When the Second World War broke out, he joined the Navy. A few years later, in 1945, he joined the air force. He became a pilot, then an instructor.

In 1958, NASA (National Aeronautics and Space Administration) was created, and announced a program to send a man into space (in earth orbit to be precise). NASA recruited the first astronauts among military pilots.

Alan Shepard was one of the selected pilots, and was finally chosen to be the first American to go into space.

On May 5, 1961, Alan Shepard takes off. His flight is shorter than Gagarin's and lasts 15 minutes. But Shepard pilots his capsule, by managing in particular the altitude, whereas Gagarin was in automatic pilot. Finally, Shepard does not eject from his capsule, but realizes a water landing (he lands on the sea).

Following this voyage, Alan Shepard becomes responsible for the training of the future American astronauts.
In 1971, he made a second trip into space and even landed on the moon (but it was not his first!).

In 1996, Alan Shepard died of leukemia.

Since then, there have been many other astronauts (men and women) who have gone into space. Some of them died in accidents, either during training, during take-off, or on their return to Earth.

MAN ON THE MOON

On July 20, 1969, an American space capsule landed on the moon for the first time.

It was the Apollo 11 mission. The United States had already sent spacecraft in orbit around the moon, but none of them had landed.

This mission consists in landing a lunar module named Eagle (a kind of small spacecraft) on the moon, then to make it take off again to join the Earth.

On July 16, 1969, three astronauts took off towards the moon. They are Neil Armstrong, Buzz Aldrin, and Michael Collins.

On July 19, the spaceship puts itself in orbit around the moon.

The following day, Neil Armstrong and Buzz Aldrin go up in the lunar module and begin their descent towards the surface of the moon. Michael Collins remains in the main spacecraft (named Columbia) which is in orbit.

The module lands on the moon. Armstrong and Aldrin begin to prepare their exit.

On July 21 at 2:56 am (universal time, also called UTC or GMT), Neil Armstrong leaves the module and puts the foot on the moon. He pronounces then this very famous sentence: " That's a one small step for a man, one giant leap for mankind ".
15 minutes later, Buzz Aldrin joined him.

Neil and Buzz take lunar soil samples, take pictures and install various measuring instruments. They go up then in the module and sleep a few hours.

They spend in all 21 hours on the moon.

98

The module then takes off and attaches itself to the spacecraft in orbit, where Michael Collins is waiting for them. Once Neil and Buzz have joined the main ship, they detach the lunar module (which will later crash on the moon).

The three astronauts then begin their return towards the Earth.

On July 24, Neil Armstrong, Buzz Aldrin, and Michael Collins land safely in the Pacific Ocean, and are recovered by helicopters of the American army.

There have been 6 trips to land on the moon. The last one took place in 1972. In total, 12 men, all Americans, have walked on the moon.

WEIGHTLESSNESS

If we watch videos of astronauts in space, we have the impression that they are floating. **This phenomenon is called weightlessness. But in reality, astronauts do not float, they fall!**

On Earth, gravity holds us down, exerting a downward force. We feel this force at all times, as our bodies push against the ground.

Our weight is defined by this gravitational force, which itself is different on each planet.
This means that our weight will be different if we go to another planet. For example, if I weigh 50 kg (110 lbs) on Earth, I will weigh 125 kg (275 lbs) on Jupiter, because Jupiter's gravitational force is stronger than Earth's.

Let's go back to Earth. If we jump out of an airplane, we fall back to the ground. And if we closed our eyes during this jump, we would still feel our fall (for example, we would feel the friction of the air on our skin).

In space, it's different. There is no air, and there is no ground. When an astronaut is in space, around the Earth, he or she feels like he or she is floating.

But if the astronaut is in free fall, why doesn't he fall to Earth?
It is a bit the same phenomenon as for the Moon. The astronaut is subject to the Earth's attraction, but his speed of movement around the Earth maintains an orbital trajectory.

When astronauts are in a space station (such as NASA's International Space Station ISS), they are also subject to weightlessness.

100

In this case, the astronauts are also in free fall, but so is the station. They are therefore weightless inside the station.

On Earth, it is possible to recreate weightlessness.

If we go up in an airplane, and that this one goes up very high in the sky then falls down towards the ground at high speed, we will be in weightlessness during the duration of the fall. Our body falling at the same speed as the plane, there will be no air friction on our skin.
The same thing happens if we take an elevator which, once we reach the top of a tower, would fall back to the ground.
Finally, some rides in amusement parks can recreate this feeling of weightlessness for a few seconds.

When they are in their space station, astronauts sometimes perform amusing experiments: If they throw a balloon, it doesn't fall back down and "floats" in the station.
But the most amusing thing is the water! If an astronaut spills water, it forms a ball and remains suspended in the station. There are videos on the Internet of these experiments.

ROCKETS

To send men or satellites into space, you need a rocket.

As we have seen, rockets were developed after the Second World War, based on the German V2 missiles. The technology of these missiles came from the work of Hermann Oberth, an Austro-Hungarian scientist, who succeeded in launching the first liquid combustion rocket in 1935.

Before that, in 1903, the Russian scientist Constantin Tsiolkovski had imagined a rocket as we know them today. Although the technology of the time did not allow the construction of such a device, Constantine had made a precise diagram of the different parts of a modern rocket.

For a rocket to take off, it needs a lot of power. To put it simply, when the fuel ignites (this is combustion), it produces a large quantity of gas which is projected backwards producing a strong thrust.

A rocket must reach a high speed to reach its orbit. And to reach this speed, it must be as light as possible. This is why rockets have several stages. Most have 3, but some have 4 or 5.

In the 16th century, a Chinese man named WAN HU tried an experiment to reach the moon. He built a chair equipped with 47 small powder rockets (like those used for fireworks). Wan Hu hoped to take off by lighting all the rockets at the same time. The experiment ended in an explosion and Wan Hu's death.

The first stage (at the bottom of the rocket) is the first engine that allows the rocket to take off. When the fuel of this stage is exhausted, this part detaches from the rocket (and falls back to Earth). Sometimes, this stage is also equipped with boosters, in order to bring even more thrust to the takeoff.

The engine of the second stage ignites and allows the rocket to accelerate, since it is lighter.

When all the stages are detached, only the fairing remains.

The nose cone can contain a satellite, or a small spacecraft containing a crew of astronauts. Some rockets also have a shuttle, which is used by astronauts to return to earth.

In RED: Booster

In YELLOW: 1st stage

In BLUE: 2nd stage

In GREEN: Nose cone

In PINK: Shuttle

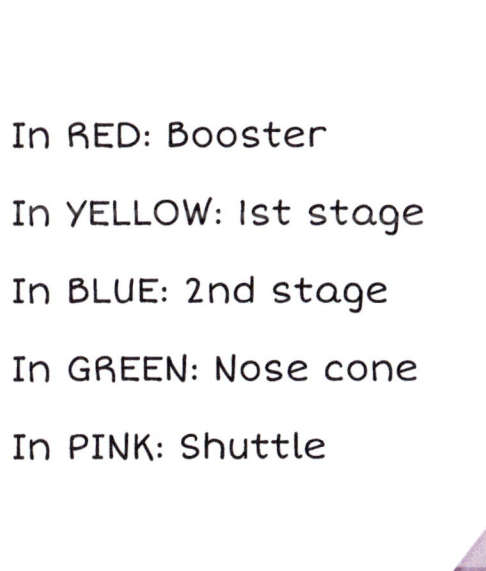

THE FUTURE OF MANKIND

The exploration of space by mankind is still in its infancy. However, it has already allowed many advances and innovations.

Of course, we have developed rockets and satellites, but space travel also allows us to experiment and develop many things in technology, biology and medicine.

Our satellites also allow us to observe our planet, and to measure the consequences of human activity, such as global warming for example. We must not forget that we do not have a backup planet at the moment.

We have discovered more than 200 planets outside our solar system, and it is possible that some of them (about ten according to NASA) are habitable. But the closest one is 40 light years away. Currently, it would take us millions of years to reach it!

On the scale of the universe, our planet is only a small grain of sand, but on a human scale, it is our one and only home.

We all need to take care of our Earth, if we want to continue stargazing for a long time.